About the Author

DALE CARNEGIE rose from the obscurity of a Missouri farm to international fame because he found a way to fill a universal human need.

It was a need that he first recognized back in 1906. At that time, young Dale Carnegie was in his junior year at State Teachers College in Warrensburg, Mo. To get an education, he was struggling against many odds. His family was poor. His Dad couldn't afford the board at college, so Dale had to ride horseback six miles each way to attend classes. Study had to be done between his farm chores. He withdrew from many school activities because he didn't have the time or the clothes. He had only one good suit. He tried for the football squad, but the coach turned him down for being too light. During this period Dale Carnegie was slowly developing an inferiority complex, the complex that could prevent him from achieving his real potential. Dale's mother knew this and suggested that he join the debating team. She knew that practice in speaking could give him the confidence and recognition that he needed.

Dale took his mother's advice, tried for the team and after several attempts finally made it. This proved to be a turning point in his life. Speaking before groups did help him gain the confidence and assurance he needed. Within a year he was winning debating contests and was on his way to garnering laurels in all the speech departments of State Teachers College. By the time Dale Carnegie was a senior, he had won every top honor in speech. Now other students were coming to him for coaching and they, in turn, were winning contests.

Out of this early struggle to overcome his feelings of inferiority, Dale Carnegie came to understand that the ability to express an idea to an audience of one or one hundred builds a person's confidence. And, with confidence, Dale Carnegie knew he could do anything he wanted to do—and so could others.

It was from this idea that Dale Carnegie developed the course that Lowell Thomas calls "the greatest movement in adult education that the world has ever known."

After college, Dale Carnegie found an attractive offer awaiting him in selling. He accepted and within a short time was highly successful. Despite his growing reputation for breaking quota records, he quit his selling career after a relatively brief period. He quit because as time went on he knew he had to test his idea that effective speaking could give a man the confidence he needed to make the most of his latent abilities. It was with this idea that Dale Carnegie headed for New York.

Two weeks after leaving Warrensburg, he was talking to the directors of the 23rd Street Y.M.C.A. in Manhattan. Dale Carnegie thought that the "Y" would be a good starting point for his course. The directors didn't think so. Flatly, they said that the "Y" couldn't afford to pay him the regular $2.00 teaching fee for a course that was untried, unknown. But when he persisted and offered to organize and teach the course on a commission basis, the directors agreed to let him give it a try.

On October 22, 1912, Dale Carnegie started his first class. Within months, the course proved so popular that the "Y" directors, instead of paying him the regular $2.00-a-night fee, were paying him $30.00 a night in commissions.

Y.M.C.A. directors in adjacent cities heard of the success that Dale Carnegie was having in New York and wanted this course in their adult education programs. Then other service clubs swelled the demand and before long Dale Carnegie was working day and night teaching the principles that a few years before had gone unrecognized and unwanted.

During this period, Dale Carnegie was introducing human-relations principles into his course. In addition to being able to speak effectively, he knew that people wanted to learn how to live and work more harmoniously with others. He was steadily researching and writing on this subject. He put his principles into booklets, and they were eagerly read and practiced by his students.

In 1933, Leon Shimkin, president of Simon and Schuster, Inc., enrolled in the course in Larchmont, N.Y. He was impressed not only with the speaking aspects of the training but with the benefits of the human-relations principles. He saw great possibilities for a book. He suggested to Dale Carnegie that he gather all the material he had been teaching his students and adapt it for a book.

On November 12, 1936, *How to Win Friends and Influence People* was published, and it became an overnight success. Dale Carnegie became a name known in every household. The book sold over a million copies in less than a year and was printed abroad in fourteen languages. For ten years it stayed on *The New York Times*' best-seller list, an all-time record for any book. Today, more than two decades after its publication, it is still selling over 250,000 copies a year and has topped the 8,400,000 figure.

Now, as you read and profit from this book, you'll be interested in knowing that the course from which this book was written is presented in 1,077 cities in the United States and Canada and in forty-five countries abroad. This vast educational system is headed by Dale Carnegie's widow, Dorothy, who helped him build the course and establish it around the globe.

For information regarding the availability of the Dale Carnegie Courses in your area, consult your telephone book or write to Dale Carnegie & Associates, Inc., (Dept. A), 1475 Franklin Avenue, Garden City, New York 11530.

Books by Dale Carnegie

How to Develop Self-Confidence and Influence
  People by Public Speaking
How to Enjoy Your Life and Your Job
How to Stop Worrying and Start Living
How to Win Friends and Influence People
The Quick and Easy Way to Effective
  Speaking

Published by POCKET BOOKS

HOW TO WIN
FRIENDS
and
Influence People

BY DALE CARNEGIE B.Pd., B.C.S., F.R.G.S., Litt.D.

Author of HOW TO STOP WORRYING AND START LIVING

PUBLISHED BY POCKET BOOKS NEW YORK

POCKET BOOKS, a Simon & Schuster division of
GULF & WESTERN CORPORATION
1230 Avenue of the Americas, New York, N.Y. 10020

ISBN: 0-671-42418-1

First Pocket Books printing August, 1940

120   119   118   117   116   115   114   113

Contents

Part I | *Fundamental Techniques in Handling People*

Part II | *Six Ways to Make People Like You*

Part III | *Twelve Ways to Win People to Your Way of Thinking*

Part IV | Nine Ways to Change People Without Giving Offense or Arousing Resentment

Part V | Letters That Produce Miraculous Results

Part VI | Seven Rules For Making Your Home Life Happier

A Short-cut to Distinction

By Lowell Thomas

ON A COLD, winter night in January, two thousand five hundred men and women thronged into the grand ballroom of the Hotel Pennsylvania in New York. Every available seat was filled by half past seven. At eight o'clock, the eager crowd was still pouring in. The spacious balcony was soon jammed; presently even standing space was at a premium and hundreds of people, tired after navigating a day in business, stood up for an hour and a half that night to witness—what?

A fashion show?

A six-day bicycle race or a personal appearance of Clark Gable?

No. These people had been lured there by a newspaper ad. Two evenings previously, they had picked up a copy of the New York *Sun* and found a full-page announcement staring them in the face.

> "INCREASE YOUR INCOME
> LEARN TO SPEAK EFFECTIVELY
> PREPARE FOR LEADERSHIP"

Old stuff? Yes, but believe it or not, in the most sophisticated town on earth, during a depression with twenty per cent of the population on relief, twenty-five hundred people left their homes and hustled to the Pennsylvania Hotel in response to that ad.

1

And the ad appeared—remember this—not in a tabloid sheet, but in the most conservative evening paper in town —the New York *Sun;* and the people who responded were of the upper economic strata—executives, employers, and professional men with incomes ranging from ten thousand to fifty thousand a year.

These men and women had come to hear the opening gun of an ultra-modern, ultra-practical course in "Effective Speaking and Influencing Men in Business"—a course given by the Dale Carnegie Institute of Effective Speaking and Human Relations.

Why were they there, these two thousand five hundred business men and women?

Because of a sudden hunger for more education due to the depression?

Apparently not, for this same course had been playing to packed houses in New York City every season for the past twenty-four years. During that time, more than fifteen thousand business and professional men had been trained by Dale Carnegie. Even large, skeptical, conservative organizations such as the Westinghouse Electric & Manufacturing Company, McGraw-Hill Publishing Company, Brooklyn Union Gas Company, Brooklyn Chamber of Commerce, American Institute of Electrical Engineers, and the New York Telephone Company have had this training conducted in their own offices for the benefit of their members and executives.

The fact that these men, ten or twenty years after leaving grade school, high school, or college, come and take this training is a glaring commentary on the shocking deficiencies of our educational system.

What do adults really want to study? That is an important question; and, in order to answer it, the University of Chicago, the American Association for Adult Education, and the United Y.M.C.A. Schools made a survey that cost $25,000 and covered two years.

That survey revealed that the prime interest of adults is health. It also revealed that their second interest is in developing skill in human relationships; they want to learn the technique of getting along with and influencing other people. They don't want to become public speakers; and they don't want to listen to a lot of high-sounding talk about psychology—they want suggestions that they can use immediately in business, in social contacts, and in the home.

So that was what adults wanted to study, was it?

"All right," said the people making the survey. "Fine. If that is what they want, we'll give it to them."

Looking around for a textbook, they discovered that no working manual had ever been written to help people solve their daily problems in human relationships.

Here was a fine kettle of fish! For hundreds of years, learned volumes had been written on Greek and Latin and higher mathematics—topics about which the average adult doesn't give two hoots. But on the one subject on which he has a thirst for knowledge, a veritable passion for guidance and help—nothing!

This explains the presence of twenty-five hundred eager adults crowding into the grand ballroom of the Hotel Pennsylvania in response to a newspaper advertisement. Here, apparently, at last was the thing for which they had long been seeking.

Back in high school and college, they had pored over books, believing that knowledge alone was the open sesame to financial and professional rewards.

But a few years in the rough-and-tumble of business and professional life had brought sharp disillusionment. They had seen some of the most important business successes won by men who possessed, in addition to their knowledge, the ability to talk well, win people to their way of thinking, and "sell" themselves and their ideas.

They soon discovered that if one aspired to wear the captain's cap and navigate the ship of business, personality and the ability to talk are more important than a knowledge of Latin verbs or a sheepskin from Harvard.

The advertisement in the New York *Sun* promised that the meeting in the Hotel Pennsylvania would be highly entertaining. It was.

Eighteen men who had taken the course were marshaled in front of the loud speaker—and each of fifteen of them was given precisely seventy-five seconds to tell his story. Only seventy-five seconds of talk, then "bang" went the gavel, and the chairman shouted, "Time! Next speaker!"

The affair moved with the speed of a herd of buffalo thundering across the plains. Spectators stood for an hour and a half to watch the performance.

The speakers were a cross section of American business life: a chain-store executive; a baker; the president of a trade association; two bankers; a truck salesman; a chemical salesman; an insurance man; the secretary of a brick manufacturers' association; an accountant; a dentist; an architect; a whiskey salesman; a Christian Science practitioner; a druggist who had come from Indianapolis to New York to take the course; a lawyer who had come from Havana, in order to prepare himself to give one important three-minute speech.

The first speaker bore the Gaelic name of Patrick J. O'Haire. Born in Ireland, he attended school for only four years, drifted to America, worked as a mechanic, then as a chauffeur.

At forty, his family was growing up, he needed more money; so he tried to sell automobile trucks. Suffering from an inferiority complex that, as he put it, was eating his heart out, he had to walk up and down in front of an office half a dozen times before he could summon up enough courage to open the door. He was so discouraged as a salesman that he was thinking of going back to work with his hands in a machine shop, when one day he received a letter inviting him to an organization meeting of the Dale Carnegie Course in Effective Speaking.

He didn't want to attend. He feared he would have to associate with a lot of college men, that he would be out of place.

His despairing wife insisted that he go, saying, "It may do you some good, Pat. God knows you need it." He went down to the place where the meeting was to be held and stood on the sidewalk for five minutes before he could generate enough self-confidence to enter the room.

The first few times he tried to speak, he was dizzy with fear. As the weeks drifted by, he lost all fear of audiences and soon found that he loved to talk—the bigger the crowd, the better. And he also lost his fear of individuals. He lost his fear of his own customers. His income mounted and skyrocketed. Today he is one of the star salesmen in New York City. That night at the Pennsylvania Hotel, Patrick O'Haire stood in front of two thousand five hundred people and told a gay, rollicking story of his achievements. Wave after wave of laughter swept over the audience. Few professional speakers could have equaled his performance.

The next speaker, Godfrey Meyer, was a grayheaded banker, the father of eleven children. The first time he attempted to speak in class, he was literally struck dumb. His mind refused to function. His story is a vivid illustration of how leadership gravitates to the man who can talk.

He works on Wall Street and for twenty-five years he has been living in Clifton, New Jersey. During that time, he had taken no active part in community affairs and knew perhaps five hundred people.

Shortly after he had enrolled in the Carnegie Course, he received his tax bill and was infuriated at what he considered unjust charges. Ordinarily, he would have sat at home and fumed, or taken it out in grousing to his neighbors. But instead, he put on his hat that night, walked into town meeting, and blew off his steam in public.

As a result of that talk of indignation, the citizens of Clifton, New Jersey, urged him to run for the town council. So for weeks he went from one meeting to another, denouncing waste and municipal extravagance.

There were ninety-six candidates in the field. When the ballots were counted, lo, Godfrey Meyer's name led all the rest. Almost overnight, he became a public figure among the forty thousand people in his community. As a result of his talks, he made eighty times more friends in six weeks than he had been able to do previously in twenty-five years.

And his salary as councilman meant that he got a return of one thousand per cent a year on his investment.

The third speaker, the head of a large national association of food manufacturers, told how he had been unable to stand up and express his ideas at meetings of a board of directors.

As a result of learning to think on his feet, two astonishing things happened. He was soon made president of his association and, in that capacity, he was obliged to address meetings all over the United States. Excerpts from his talks were put on the Associated Press wires and printed in newspapers and trade magazines throughout the country.

In two years, after learning to speak, he received more free publicity for his company and its products than he had been able to get previously by a quarter of a million dollars spent in direct advertising. This speaker admitted that he had formerly hesitated to telephone some of the more important executives in lower Manhattan and invite them to lunch with him. But as a result of the prestige he had acquired by his talks, these same men now telephoned him and invited him to lunch and apologized to him for encroaching on his time.

The ability to speak is a short-cut to distinction. It puts a man in the limelight, raises him head and shoulders above the crowd. And the man who can speak acceptably is usually given credit for an ability out of all proportion to what he really possesses.

A movement for adult education is sweeping over the nation today; and the most spectacular force in that movement is Dale Carnegie, a man who has listened to and criticized more talks by adults than has any other man in captivity. According to a recent cartoon by "Believe-It-or-Not" Ripley, he has criticized 150,000 speeches. If that grand total doesn't impress you, remember that it means one talk for almost every day that has passed since Columbus discovered America. Or, to put it in other words, if all the men who have spoken before him had used only three minutes and had appeared before him in succession, it would have taken a solid year, listening day and night, to hear them all.

Dale Carnegie's own career, filled with sharp contrasts, is a striking example of what a man can accomplish when he is obsessed with an original idea and afire with enthusiasm.

Born on a Missouri farm ten miles from a railway, he never saw a street car until he was twelve years old; yet, at forty-six, he was familiar with the far-flung corners of the earth, everywhere from Hong Kong to Hammerfest; and, at one time, he approached closer to the North Pole than Admiral Byrd's headquarters at Little America were to the South Pole.

This Missouri lad who once picked strawberries and cut cockleburs for five cents an hour is now paid a dollar a minute for training the executives of large corporations in the art of self-expression.

This erstwhile cowboy who once punched cattle and branded calves and rode fences out in western South Dakota later went to London and put on shows under the patronage of His Royal Highness, the Prince of Wales.

This chap who was a total failure the first half-dozen times that he tried to speak in public later became my personal manager. Much of my success has been due to training under Dale Carnegie.

Young Carnegie had to struggle for an education, for hard luck was always battering away at the old farm in northwest Missouri with a flying tackle and a body slam. Year after year, the "102" River rose and drowned the corn and swept away the hay. Season after season, the fat hogs sickened and died from cholera, the bottom fell out of the market for cattle and mules, and the bank threatened to foreclose the mortgage.

Sick with discouragement, the family sold out and bought another farm near the State Teachers College at Warrensburg, Missouri. Board and room could be had in town for a dollar a day; but young Carnegie couldn't afford it. So he stayed on the farm and commuted on horseback three miles to college each day. At home, he milked the cows, cut the wood, fed the hogs, and studied his Latin verbs by the light of a coal-oil lamp until his eyes blurred and he began to nod.

Even when he got to bed at midnight, he set the alarm for three o'clock. His father bred pedigreed Duroc-Jersey hogs—and there was danger, during the bitter cold nights, of the young pigs' freezing to death; so they were put in a basket, covered with a gunny sack, and set behind the kitchen stove. True to their nature, the pigs demanded a hot meal at three A.M. So when the alarm went off, Dale Carnegie crawled out of the blankets, took the basket of pigs out to their mother, waited for them to nurse, and then brought them back to the warmth of the kitchen stove.

There were six hundred students in State Teachers College; and Dale Carnegie was one of the isolated half dozen who couldn't afford to board in town. He was ashamed of the poverty that made it necessary for him to ride back to the farm and milk the cows every night. He was ashamed of his coat, which was too tight, and his trousers, which were too short. Rapidly developing an inferiority complex, he looked about for some short-cut to distinction. He soon saw that there were certain groups in college that enjoyed influence and prestige—the football and baseball players and the chaps who won the debating and public-speaking contests.

Realizing that he had no flair for athletics, he decided to win one of the speaking contests. He spent months preparing his talks. He practiced as he sat in the saddle galloping to college and back; he practiced his speeches as he milked the cows; and then he mounted a bale of hay in the barn and with great gusto and gestures harangued the frightened pigeons about the necessity of halting Japanese immigration.

But in spite of all his earnestness and preparation, he met with defeat after defeat. He was eighteen at the time—sensitive and proud. He became so discouraged, so depressed that he even thought of suicide. And then suddenly he began to win, not one contest but every speaking contest in college.

Other students pleaded with him to train them; and they won also.

Graduating from college, he started selling correspondence courses to the ranchers among the sand hills of western Nebraska and eastern Wyoming.

In spite of all his boundless energy and enthusiasm, he couldn't make the grade. He became so discouraged that he went to his hotel room in Alliance, Nebraska, in the middle of the day, threw himself across the bed, and wept with despair. He longed to go back to college, he longed to retreat from the harsh battle of life; but he couldn't. So he resolved to go to Omaha and get another job. He didn't have the money for a railroad ticket so he traveled on a freight train, feeding and watering two carloads of wild horses in return for his passage. Landing in South Omaha, he got a job selling bacon and soap and lard for Armour and Company. His territory was up among the Bad Lands and the cow and Indian country of western South Dakota. He covered his territory by freight train and on stage coach and on horseback and slept in pioneer hotels where the only partition between the rooms was a sheet of muslin. He studied books on salesmanship, rode bucking broncos, played poker with squaw men, and learned how to collect money. When an inland storekeeper couldn't pay cash for the bacon and hams he had ordered, Dale Carnegie would take a dozen pairs of shoes off his shelf, sell the shoes to the railroad men, and forward the receipts to Armour and Company.

He would often ride a freight train a hundred miles a day. When the train stopped to unload freight, he would dash uptown, see three or four merchants, get his orders; and when the whistle blew, he would dash down the street again lickety-split and swing onto the train while it was moving.

Within two years, he had taken an unproductive territory that stood in the twenty-fifth place and boosted it to first place among all the twenty-nine car routes leading out of South Omaha. Armour and Company offered to promote him, saying: "You have achieved what seemed impossible." But he refused the promotion and resigned—resigned, went to New York, studied at the American Academy of Dramatic Arts, and toured the country playing the role of Dr. Hartley in *Polly of the Circus*.

He would never be a Booth or a Barrymore. He had the good sense to recognize that. So back he went to sales work again, dispensing automobile trucks for the Packard Motor Car Company.

He knew nothing about machinery and cared nothing about it. Dreadfully unhappy, he had to scourge himself to his task each day. He longed to have time to study, to write the books he had dreamed about writing back in college. So he resigned. He was going to spend his days writing stories and novels and support himself by teaching in a night school.

Teaching what? As he looked back and evaluated his college work, he saw that his training in public speaking had done more to give him confidence, courage, poise, and the ability to meet and deal with people in business than had all the rest of his college courses put together. So he urged the Y.M.C.A. schools in New York to give him a chance to conduct courses in public speaking for business men.

What? Make orators out of business men? Absurd. They knew. They had tried such courses—and they had always failed.

When they refused to pay him a salary of two dollars a night, he agreed to teach on a commission basis and take a percentage of the net profits—if there were any profits to take. And inside of three years they were paying him thirty dollars a night on that basis—instead of two.

The course grew. Other "Y's" heard of it, then other cities. Dale Carnegie soon became a glorified circuit rider covering New York, Philadelphia, Baltimore, and later London and Paris. All the textbooks were too academic and impractical for the business men who flocked to his courses. Nothing daunted, he sat down and wrote one entitled *Public Speaking and Influencing Men in Business*. It is now the official text of all the Y.M.C.A.'s as well as the American Bankers' Association and the National Credit Men's Association.

Today far more adults come to Dale Carnegie for training in public speaking each season than go to all the extension courses in public speaking conducted by all the twenty-two colleges and universities located in New York City.

Dale Carnegie claims that any man can talk when he gets mad. He says that if you hit the most ignorant man in town on the jaw and knock him down, he will get on his feet and talk with an eloquence, heat, and emphasis that would have rivaled William Jennings Bryan in his palmiest days. He claims that almost any man can speak acceptably in public if he has self-confidence and an idea that is boiling and stewing within him.

The way to develop self-confidence, he says, is to do the thing you fear to do and get a record of successful experiences behind you. So he forces each man to talk at every session of the course. The audience is sympathetic. They are all in the same boat; and, by constant practice, they develop a courage, confidence, and enthusiasm that carry over into their private speaking.

Dale Carnegie will tell you that he has made a living all these years, not by teaching public speaking—that has been incidental. He claims his main job has been to help men conquer their fears and develop courage.

He started out at first to conduct merely a course in public speaking, but the students who came were business men. Many of them hadn't seen the inside of a classroom in thirty years. Most of them were paying their tuition on the installment plan. They wanted results and they wanted them quick—results that they could use the next day in business interviews and in speaking before groups.

So he was forced to be swift and practical. Consequently, he has developed a system of training that is unique—a striking combination of public speaking, salesmanship, human relations, and applied psychology.

A slave to no hard and fast rules, he has developed a course that is as real as the measles and twice as much fun.

When the classes terminate, the men form clubs of their own and continue to meet fortnightly for years afterwards. One group of nineteen men in Philadelphia has been meeting twice a month during the winter season for seventeen years. Men frequently motor fifty or a hundred miles to attend these classes. One student used to commute each week from Chicago to New York.

Professor William James of Harvard used to say that the average man develops only ten per cent of his latent mental ability. Dale Carnegie, by helping business men and women to develop their latent possibilities, has created one of the most significant movements in adult education.

How This Book Was Written— and Why

By Dale Carnegie

DURING THE LAST thirty-five years, the publishing houses of America have printed more than a fifth of a million different books. Most of them were deadly dull; and many were financial failures. "Many," did I say? The president of one of the largest publishing houses in the world recently confessed to me that his company, after seventy-five years of publishing experience, still loses money on seven out of every eight books it publishes.

Why, then, have I had the temerity to write another book? And, after I have written it, why should you bother to read it?

Fair questions, both; and I'll try to answer them.

In order to explain precisely how and why this book was written, I may, unfortunately, have to repeat briefly some of the facts that you have already read in Lowell Thomas' introduction entitled "A Short-Cut to Distinction."

I have, since 1912, been conducting educational courses for business and professional men and women in New York. At first, I conducted courses in public speaking only —courses designed to train adults, by actual experience, to think on their feet and express their ideas with more clarity, more effectiveness, and more poise, both in business interviews and before groups.

But gradually, as the seasons passed, I realized that sorely as these adults needed training in effective speaking, they needed still more training in the fine art of getting along with people in everyday business and social contacts.

I also gradually realized that I was sorely in need of such training myself. As I look back now across the years, I am appalled at my own frequent lack of finesse and understanding. How I wish a book such as this had been placed in my hands twenty years ago! What a priceless boon it would have been!

Dealing with people is probably the biggest problem you face, especially if you are a business man. Yes, and that is also true if you are a housewife, architect, or engineer. Research made a few years ago under the auspices of the Carnegie Foundation for the Advancement of Teachers uncovered a most important and significant fact—a fact later confirmed by additional studies made at the Carnegie Institute of Technology. These investigations revealed that even in such technical lines as engineering, about 15 per cent of one's financial success is due to one's technical knowledge and about 85 per cent is due to skill in human engineering—to personality and the ability to lead people.

For many years, I conducted courses each season in the Engineers' Club of Philadelphia, and also courses for the New York Chapter of the American Institute of Electrical Engineers. A total of probably more than 1,500 engineers have passed through my classes. They came to me because they finally realized, after years of observation and experience, that the highest-paid men in the engineering field are frequently not the men who know most about engineering. One can, for example, hire mere technical ability in engineering, accountancy, architecture or any other profession at fifty to seventy-five dollars a week. The market is always glutted with it. But the man who has technical knowledge *plus* the ability to express his ideas, to assume leadership, and to arouse enthusiasm among men—that man is headed for higher earning power.

In the heyday of his activity, John D. Rockefeller told Matthew C. Brush that "the ability to deal with people is as purchasable a commodity as sugar or coffee." "And I will pay more for that ability," said John D., "than for any other under the sun."

Wouldn't you suppose that every college in the land would conduct courses to develop the highest-priced ability under the sun? But if there is just one practical, common-sense course of that kind given for adults in even one college in the land, it has escaped my attention up to the present writing.

The University of Chicago and the United Y.M.C.A. Schools conducted a survey to determine what adults really want to study.

That survey cost $25,000 and took two years. The last part of the survey was made in Meriden, Connecticut. It was taken as a typical American town. Every adult in Meriden was interviewed and requested to answer 156 questions—questions such as "What is your business or profession? Your education? How do you spend your spare time? What is your income? Your hobbies? Your ambitions? Your problems? What subjects are you most interested in studying?" And so on. That survey revealed that health is the prime interest of adults—and that their second interest is people: how to understand and get along with people; how to make people like you; and how to win others to your way of thinking.

So the committee conducting this survey resolved to conduct such a course for adults in Meriden. They searched diligently for a practical textbook on the subject but found —not one. Finally they approached one of the world's outstanding authorities on adult education and asked him if he knew of any book which met the needs of this group. "No," he replied, "I know what those adults want. But the book they need has never been written."

I knew from experience that this statement was true, for I myself had been searching for years to discover a practical, working handbook on human relations.

Since no such book existed, I have tried to write one for use in my own courses. And here it is. I hope you like it.

In preparation for this book, I read everything that I could find on the subject—everything from Dorothy Dix, the divorce-court records, and the *Parents' Magazine,* to Professor Overstreet, Alfred Adler, and William James. In addition to that, I hired a trained research man to spend

one and a half years in various libraries reading everything
I had missed, plowing through erudite tomes on psychology, poring over hundreds of magazine articles, searching
through countless biographies, trying to ascertain how the
great men of all ages had dealt with people. We read the
biographies of the great men of all ages. We read the life
stories of all great leaders from Julius Caesar to Thomas
Edison. I recall that we read over one hundred biographies
of Theodore Roosevelt alone. We were determined to spare
no time, no expense, to discover every practical idea that
anyone had ever used throughout the ages to win friends
and influence people.

I personally interviewed scores of successful people,
some of them world-famous—Marconi, Franklin D. Roosevelt, Owen D. Young, Clark Gable, Mary Pickford, Martin
Johnson—and tried to discover the technique they used in
human relations.

From all this material, I prepared a short talk. I called
it "How to Win Friends and Influence People." I say
"short." It *was* short in the beginning, but it has now expanded to a lecture that consumes one hour and thirty minutes. For years, I have given this talk each season to the
adults in the Carnegie Institute courses in New York.

I gave the talk and urged them to go out and test it in
their business and social contacts, and then come back to
class and speak about their experiences and the results they
had achieved. What an interesting assignment! These men
and women, hungry for self-improvement, were fascinated
by the idea of working in a new kind of laboratory—the
first and only laboratory of human relationships for adults
that has ever existed.

This book wasn't written in the usual sense of the word.
It grew as a child grows. It grew and developed out of that
laboratory, out of the experiences of thousands of adults.

Years ago, we started with a set of rules printed on a
card no larger than a post card. The next season we printed
a larger card, then a leaflet, then a series of booklets, each
one expanding in size and scope. And now, after fifteen
years of experiment and research, comes this book.

The rules we have set down here are not mere theories

or guess work. They work like magic. Incredible as it sounds, I have seen the application of these principles literally revolutionize the lives of many people.

To illustrate: Last season a man with 314 employees joined one of these courses. For years, he had driven and criticized and condemned his employees without stint or discretion. Kindness, words of appreciation, and encouragement were alien to his lips. After studying the principles discussed in this book, this employer sharply altered his philosophy of life. His organization is now inspired with a new loyalty, a new enthusiasm, a new spirit of team work. Three hundred and fourteen enemies have been turned into three hundred and fourteen friends. As he proudly said in a speech before the class: "When I used to walk through my establishment, no one greeted me. My employees actually looked the other way when they saw me approaching. But now they are all my friends and even the janitor calls me by my first name."

This employer now has more profit, more leisure, and— what is infinitely more important—he finds far more happiness in his business and in his home.

Countless numbers of salesmen have sharply increased their sales by the use of these principles. Many have opened up new accounts—accounts that they had formerly solicited in vain. Executives have been given increased authority, increased pay. One executive last season reported an increase in salary of five thousand a year largely because he applied these truths. Another, an executive in the Philadelphia Gas Works Company, was slated for demotion because of his belligerence, because of his inability to lead people skillfully. This training not only saved him from a demotion when he was sixty-five, but it brought him promotion with increased pay.

On innumerable occasions, wives attending the banquet given at the end of the course have told me that their homes have been much happier since their husbands took this training.

Men are frequently astonished at the new results they achieve. It all seems like magic. In some cases, in their enthusiasm, they have telephoned me at my home on Sundays because they couldn't wait forty-eight hours to report their achievements at the regular session of the course.

One man was so stirred by a talk on these principles last season that he sat discussing them with the other members of the class until far into the night. At three o'clock in the morning, the others went home. But he was so shaken by a realization of his own mistakes, so inspired by the vista of a new and richer world opening before him, that he was unable to sleep. He didn't sleep that night or the next day or the next night.

Who was he? A naive, untrained individual ready to gush over any new theory that came along? No. Far from it. He is a sophisticated, blasé dealer in art, very much the man about town, who speaks three languages fluently and is a graduate of two foreign universities.

While writing this chapter, I received a letter from a German of the old school, an aristocrat whose forbears had served for generations as professional army officers under the Hohenzollerns. His letter, written from a transatlantic steamer, telling about the application of these principles, rose almost to a religious fervor.

Another man, an old New Yorker, a Harvard graduate, whose name looms large in the Social Register, a wealthy man, the owner of a large carpet factory, declared that he had learned more in fourteen weeks through this system of training about the fine art of influencing people than he had learned about the same subject during his four years in college. Absurd? Laughable? Fantastic? Of course, you are privileged to dismiss this statement with whatever adjective you wish. I am merely reporting, without comment, a declaration made by a conservative and eminently successful Harvard graduate in a public address to approximately six hundred men at the Yale Club in New York on the evening of Thursday, February 23, 1933.

"Compared to what we ought to be," said the famous Professor William James of Harvard, "compared to what we ought to be, we are only half awake. We are making use of only a small part of our physical and mental resources. Stating the thing broadly, the human individual thus lives far within his limits. He possesses powers of various sorts which he habitually fails to use."

Those powers which you "habitually fail to use"! The sole purpose of this book is to help you discover, develop, and profit by those dormant and unused assets.

"Education," said Dr. John G. Hibben, former President of Princeton University, "education is the ability to meet life's situations."

If by the time you have finished reading the first three chapters of this book—if you aren't then a little better equipped to meet life's situations, then I shall consider this book to be a total failure, so far as you are concerned. For *"the great aim of education,"* said Herbert Spencer, *"is not knowledge but action."*

And this is an *action* book.

This introduction, like most introductions, is already too long. So let's go. Let's get down to brass tacks at once. Please turn immediately to Chapter One.

PART ONE

Fundamental Techniques in Handling People

CHAPTER ONE

"If You Want to Gather Honey, Don't Kick Over the Beehive"

ON MAY 7, 1931, New York City witnessed the most sensational man-hunt the old town had ever known. After weeks of search, "Two Gun" Crowley—the killer, the gunman who didn't smoke or drink—was at bay, trapped in his sweetheart's apartment on West End Avenue.

One hundred and fifty policemen and detectives laid siege to his top-floor hideaway. Chopping holes in the roof, they tried to smoke out Crowley, the "cop killer," with tear gas. Then they mounted their machine guns on surrounding buildings, and for more than an hour one of New York's fine residential sections reverberated with the crack of pistol fire and the rat-tat-tat of machine guns. Crowley, crouching behind an overstuffed chair, fired incessantly at the police. Ten thousand excited people watched the battle. Nothing like it had ever been seen before on the sidewalks of New York.

When Crowley was captured, Police Commissioner Mulrooney declared that the two-gun desperado was one of the most dangerous criminals ever encountered in the history of New York. "He will kill," said the Commissioner, "at the drop of a feather."

But how did "Two Gun" Crowley regard himself? We know, because while the police were firing into his apartment, he wrote a letter addressed "To whom it may concern." And, as he wrote, the blood flowing from his wounds left a crimson trail on the paper. In this letter Crowley said: "Under my coat is a weary heart, but a kind one—one that would do nobody any harm."

A short time before this, Crowley had been having a necking party on a country road out on Long Island. Suddenly a policeman walked up to the parked car and said: "Let me see your license."

Without saying a word, Crowley drew his gun, and cut the policeman down with a shower of lead. As the dying officer fell Crowley leaped out of the car, grabbed the officer's revolver, and fired another bullet into the prostrate body. And that was the killer who said: "Under my coat is a weary heart, but a kind one—one that would do nobody any harm."

Crowley was sentenced to the electric chair. When he arrived at the death house at Sing Sing, did he say, "This is what I get for killing people?" No, he said: "This is what I get for defending myself."

The point of the story is this: "Two Gun" Crowley didn't blame himself for anything.

Is that an unusual attitude among criminals? If you think so, listen to this:

"I have spent the best years of my life giving people the lighter pleasures, helping them have a good time, and all I get is abuse, the existence of a hunted man."

That's Al Capone speaking. Yes, America's erstwhile Public Enemy Number One—the most sinister gangleader who ever shot up Chicago. Capone didn't condemn himself. He actually regarded himself as a public benefactor— an unappreciated and misunderstood public benefactor.

And so did Dutch Schultz before he crumpled up under gangsters bullets in Newark. Dutch Schultz, one of New

York's most notorious rats, said in a newspaper interview that he was a public benefactor. And he believed it.

I have had some interesting correspondence with Warden Lawes of Sing Sing on this subject, and he declares that "few of the criminals in Sing Sing regard themselves as bad men. They are just as human as you and I. So they rationalize, they explain. They can tell you why they had to crack a safe or be quick on the trigger finger. Most of them attempt by a form of reasoning, fallacious or logical, to justify their anti-social acts even to themselves, consequently stoutly maintaining that they should never have been imprisoned at all."

If Al Capone, "Two Gun" Crowley, Dutch Schultz, the desperate men behind prison walls don't blame themselves for anything—what about the people with whom you and I come in contact?

The late John Wanamaker once confessed: "I learned thirty years ago that it is foolish to scold. I have enough trouble overcoming my own limitations without fretting over the fact that God has not seen fit to distribute evenly the gift of intelligence."

Wanamaker learned this lesson early; but I personally had to blunder through this old world for a third of a century before it even began to dawn upon me that ninety-nine times out of a hundred, no man ever criticizes himself for anything, no matter how wrong he may be.

Criticism is futile because it puts a man on the defensive, and usually makes him strive to justify himself. Criticism is dangerous, because it wounds a man's precious pride, hurts his sense of importance, and arouses his resentment.

The German army won't let a soldier file a complaint and make a criticism immediately after a thing has happened. He has to sleep on his grudge first and cool off. If he files his complaint immediately, he is punished. By the eternals, there ought to be a law like that in civil life too—a law for whining parents and nagging wives and scolding employers and the whole obnoxious parade of fault-finders.

You will find examples of the futility of criticism bristling on a thousand pages of history. Take, for example, the famous quarrel between Theodore Roosevelt and President Taft—a quarrel that split the Republican Party, put Woodrow Wilson in the White House, and wrote bold, luminous lines across the World War and altered the flow of history. Let's review the facts quickly: When Theodore Roosevelt stepped out of the White House in 1908, he made Taft President, and then went off to Africa to shoot lions. When he returned, he exploded. He denounced Taft for his conservatism, tried to secure the nomination for a third term himself, formed the Bull Moose Party, and all but demolished the GOP. In the election that followed, William Howard Taft and the Republican Party carried only two states—Vermont and Utah. The most disastrous defeat the old party had ever known.

Theodore Roosevelt blamed Taft; but did President Taft blame himself? Of course not. With tears in his eyes, Taft said: "I don't see how I could have done any differently from what I have."

Who was to blame? Roosevelt or Taft? Frankly, I don't know, and I don't care. The point I am trying to make is that all of Theodore Roosevelt's criticism didn't persuade Taft that he was wrong. It merely made Taft strive to justify himself and to reiterate with tears in his eyes: "I don't see how I could have done any differently from what I have."

Or, take the Teapot Dome oil scandal. Remember it? It kept the newspapers ringing with indignation for years. It rocked the nation! Nothing like it had ever happened before in American public life within the memory of living men. Here are the bare facts of the scandal: Albert Fall, Secretary of the Interior in Harding's cabinet, was entrusted with the leasing of government oil reserves at Elk Hill and Teapot Dome—oil reserves that had been set aside for the future use of the Navy. Did Secretary Fall permit competitive bidding? No sir. He handed the fat, juicy contract outright to his friend, Edward L. Doheny. And what did Doheny do? He gave Secretary Fall what he was pleased to call a "loan" of one hundred thousand dollars. Then, in a high-handed manner, Secretary Fall ordered United States Marines into the district to drive off competitors whose adjacent wells were sapping oil out of the Elk Hill reserves. These competitors, driven off their ground at the ends of guns and bayonets, rushed into court —and blew the lid off the hundred million dollar Teapot Dome scandal. A stench arose so vile that it ruined the Harding administration, nauseated an entire nation, threatened to wreck the Republican Party, and put Albert B. Fall behind prison bars.

Fall was condemned viciously—condemned as few men in public life have ever been. Did he repent? Never! Years later Herbert Hoover intimated in a public speech that President Harding's death had been due to mental anxiety and worry because a friend had betrayed him. When Mrs. Fall heard that, she sprang from her chair, she wept, she shook her fists at fate, and screamed: "What! Harding betrayed by Fall? No! My husband never betrayed anyone. This whole house full of gold would not tempt my husband to do wrong. He is the one who has been betrayed and led to the slaughter and crucified."

There you are: human nature in action, the wrong-doer blaming everybody but himself. We are all like that. So when you and I are tempted to criticize someone tomorrow, let's remember Al Capone, "Two Gun" Crowley, and Albert Fall. Let's realize that criticisms are like homing pigeons. They always return home. Let's realize that the person we are going to correct and condemn will probably justify himself, and condemn us in return; or, like the gentle Taft, he will say: "I don't see how I could have done any differently from what I have."

On Saturday morning, April 15, 1865, Abraham Lincoln lay dying in a hall bedroom of a cheap lodging house directly across the street from Ford's Theatre, where Booth had shot him. Lincoln's long body lay stretched diagonally across a sagging bed that was too short for him. A cheap reproduction of Rosa Bonheur's famous painting, "The Horse Fair," hung above the bed, and a dismal gas jet flickered yellow light.

As Lincoln lay dying, Secretary of War Stanton said, "There lies the most perfect ruler of men that the world has ever seen."

What was the secret of Lincoln's success in dealing with men? I studied the life of Abraham Lincoln for ten years, and devoted all of three years to writing and rewriting a book entitled *Lincoln the Unknown*. I believe I have made as detailed and exhaustive a study of Lincoln's personality and home life as it is possible for any human being to make. I made a special study of Lincoln's method of dealing with men. Did he indulge in criticism? Oh, yes. As a young man in the Pigeon Creek Valley of Indiana, he not only criticized but he wrote letters and poems ridiculing people and dropped these letters on the country roads where they were sure to be found. One of these letters aroused resentments that burned for a lifetime.

Even after Lincoln had become a practicing lawyer in Springfield, Illinois, he attacked his opponents openly in letters published in the newspapers. But he did this just once too often.

In the autumn of 1842, he ridiculed a vain, pugnacious Irish politician by the name of James Shields. Lincoln lampooned him through an anonymous letter published in the *Springfield Journal*. The town roared with laughter. Shields, sensitive and proud, boiled with indignation. He found out who wrote the letter, leaped on his horse, started after Lincoln, and challenged him to fight a duel. Lincoln didn't want to fight. He was opposed to dueling; but he couldn't get out of it and save his honor. He was given the choice of weapons. Since he had very long arms, he chose cavalry broad swords, took lessons in sword fighting from a West Point graduate; and, on the appointed day, he and Shields met on a sand bar in the Mississippi River, prepared to fight to the death; but, at the last minute, their seconds interrupted and stopped the duel.

That was the most lurid personal incident in Lincoln's life. It taught him an invaluable lesson in the art of dealing with people. Never again did he write an insulting letter. Never again did he ridicule anyone. And from that time on, he almost never criticized anybody for anything.

Time after time, during the Civil War, Lincoln put a new general at the head of the Army of the Potomac, and each one in turn—McClellan, Pope, Burnside, Hooker,

Meade—blundered tragically, and drove Lincoln to pacing the floor in despair. Half the nation savagely condemned these incompetent generals, but Lincoln, "with malice towards none, with charity for all," held his peace. One of his favorite quotations was "Judge not, that ye be not judged."

And when Mrs. Lincoln and others spoke harshly of the Southern people, Lincoln replied: "Don't criticize them; they are just what we would be under similar circumstances."

Yet, if any man ever had occasion to criticize, surely it was Lincoln. Let's take just one illustration:

The Battle of Gettysburg was fought during the first three days of July, 1863. During the night of July 4, Lee began to retreat southward while storm clouds deluged the country with rain. When Lee reached the Potomac with his defeated army, he found a swollen, impassable river in front of him, and a victorious Union army behind him. Lee was in a trap. He couldn't escape. Lincoln saw that. Here was a golden, heaven-sent opportunity—the opportunity to capture Lee's army and end the war immediately. So, with a surge of high hope, Lincoln ordered Meade not to call a council of war but to attack Lee immediately. Lincoln telegraphed his orders and then sent a special messenger to Meade demanding immediate action.

And what did General Meade do? He did the very opposite of what he was told to do. He called a council of war in direct violation of Lincoln's orders. He hesitated. He procrastinated. He telegraphed all manner of excuses. He refused point blank to attack Lee. Finally the waters receded and Lee escaped over the Potomac with his forces.

Lincoln was furious. "What does this mean?" Lincoln cried to his son Robert. "Great God! What does this mean? We had them within our grasp, and had only to stretch forth our hands and they were ours; yet nothing that I could say or do could make the army move. Under the circumstances, almost any general could have defeated Lee. If I had gone up there, I could have whipped him myself."

In bitter disappointment, Lincoln sat down and wrote

Meade this letter. And remember, at this period of his life was extremely conservative and restrained in his phraseology. So this letter coming from Lincoln in 1863 was tantamount to the severest rebuke.

"My dear General,

"I do not believe you appreciate the magnitude of the misfortune involved in Lee's escape. He was within our easy grasp, and to have closed upon him would, in connection with our other late successes, have ended the war. As it is, the war will be prolonged indefinitely. If you could not safely attack Lee last Monday, how can you possibly do so south of the river, when you can take with you very few—no more than two-thirds of the force you then had in hand? It would be unreasonable to expect and I do not expect that you can now effect much. Your golden opportunity is gone, and I am distressed immeasurably because of it."

What do you suppose Meade did when he read that letter?

Meade never saw that letter. Lincoln never mailed it. It was found among Lincoln's papers after his death.

My guess is—and this is only a guess—that after writing that letter, Lincoln looked out of the window and said to himself, "Just a minute. Maybe I ought not to be so hasty. It is easy enough for me to sit here in the quiet of the White House and order Meade to attack; but if I had been up at Gettysburg, and if I had seen as much blood as Meade has seen during the last week, and if my ears had been pierced with the screams and shrieks of the wounded and dying, maybe I wouldn't be so anxious to attack either. If I had Meade's timid temperament, perhaps I would have done just what he has done. Anyhow, it is water under the bridge now. If I send this letter, it will relieve my feelings but it will make Meade try to justify himself. It will make him condemn me. It will arouse hard feelings, impair all his further usefulness as a commander, and perhaps force him to resign from the army."

So, as I have already said, Lincoln put the letter aside,

for he had learned by bitter experience that sharp criticisms and rebukes almost invariably end in futility.

Theodore Roosevelt said that when he, as President, was confronted by some perplexing problem, he used to lean back and look up at a large painting of Lincoln that hung above his desk in the White House and ask himself, "What would Lincoln do if he were in my shoes? How would he solve this problem?"

The next time we are tempted to give somebody "hail Columbia," let's pull a five-dollar bill out of our pocket, look at Lincoln's picture on the bill, and ask, "How would Lincoln handle this problem if he had it?"

Do you know someone you would like to change and regulate and improve? Good! That is fine. I am all in favor of it. But why not begin on yourself? From a purely selfish standpoint, that is a lot more profitable than trying to improve others—yes, and a lot less dangerous.

"When a man's fight begins within himself," said Browning, "he is worth something." It will probably take from now until Christmas to perfect yourself. You can then have a nice long rest over the holidays and devote the New Year to regulating and criticizing other people.

But perfect yourself first.

"Don't complain about the snow on your neighbor's roof," said Confucius, "when your own doorstep is unclean."

When I was still young and trying hard to impress people, I wrote a foolish letter to Richard Harding Davis, an author who once loomed large on the literary horizon of America. I was preparing a magazine article about authors; and I asked Davis to tell me about his method of work. A few weeks earlier, I had received a letter from someone with this notation at the bottom: "Dictated but not read." I was quite impressed. I felt the writer must be very big and busy and important. I wasn't the slightest bit busy; but I was eager to make an impression on Richard Harding Davis so I ended my short note with the words: "Dictated but not read."

He never troubled to answer the letter. He simply returned it to me with this scribbled across the bottom: "Your bad manners are exceeded only by your bad manners." True, I had blundered, and perhaps I deserved his rebuke. But, being human, I resented it. I resented it so sharply that when I read of the death of Richard Harding Davis ten years later, the one thought that still persisted in my mind—and I am ashamed to admit—was the hurt he had given me.

If you and I want to stir up a resentment tomorrow that may rankle across the decades and endure until death, just let us indulge in a little stinging criticism—no matter how certain we are that it is justified.

When dealing with people, let us remember we are not dealing with creatures of logic. We are dealing with creatures of emotion, creatures bristling with prejudices and motivated by pride and vanity.

And criticism is a dangerous spark—a spark that is liable to cause an explosion in the powder magazine of pride—an explosion that sometimes hastens death. For example, General Leonard Wood was criticized and not allowed to go with the army to France. That blow to his pride probably shortened his life.

Bitter criticism caused the sensitive Thomas Hardy, one of the finest novelists that ever enriched English literature, to give up the writing of fiction forever. Criticism drove Thomas Chatterton, the English poet, to suicide.

Benjamin Franklin, tactless in his youth, became so diplomatic, so adroit at handling people that he was made American Ambassador to France. The secret of his success? "I will speak ill of no man," he said, ". . . and speak all the good I know of everybody."

Any fool can criticize, condemn, and complain—and most fools do.

But it takes character and self-control to be understanding and forgiving.

"A great man shows his greatness," said Carlyle, "by the way he treats little men."

Instead of condemning people, let's try to understand them. Let's try to figure out why they do what they do. That's a lot more profitable and intriguing than criticism;

and it breeds sympathy, tolerance, and kindness. "To know all is to forgive all."

As Dr. Johnson said: "God Himself, sir, does not propose to judge man until the end of his days."

Why should you and I?

CHAPTER TWO

The Big Secret of Dealing with People

THERE IS ONLY ONE way under high Heaven to get anybody to do anything. Did you ever stop to think of that? Yes, just one way. And that is by making the other person want to do it.

Remember, there is no other way.

Of course, you can make a man want to give you his watch by sticking a revolver in his ribs. You can make an employee give you co-operation—until your back is turned —by threatening to fire him. You can make a child do what you want it to do by a whip or a threat. But these crude methods have sharply undesirable repercussions.

The only way I can get you to do anything is by giving you what you want.

What do you want?

The famous Dr. Sigmund Freud of Vienna, one of the most distinguished psychologists of the twentieth century, says that everything you and I do springs from two motives: the sex urge and the desire to be great.

Professor John Dewey, America's most profound philosopher, phrases it a bit differently. Dr. Dewey says the deepest urge in human nature is "the desire to be important." Remember that phrase: "the desire to be important." It is significant. You are going to hear a lot about it in this book.

What do you want? Not many things, but the few things that you do wish, you crave with an insistence that will not be denied. Almost every normal adult wants—

1. Health and the preservation of life.
2. Food.
3. Sleep.
4. Money and the things money will buy.
5. Life in the hereafter.
6. Sexual gratification.
7. The well-being of our children.
8. A feeling of importance.

Almost all these wants are gratified—all except one. But there is one longing almost as deep, almost as imperious, as the desire for food or sleep which is seldom gratified. It is what Freud calls "the desire to be great." It is what Dewey calls the "desire to be important."

Lincoln once began a letter by saying: "Everybody likes a compliment." William James said: "The deepest principle in human nature is the craving to be appreciated." He didn't speak, mind you, of the "wish" or the "desire" or the "longing" to be appreciated. He said the *"craving"* to be appreciated.

Here is a gnawing and unfaltering human hunger; and the rare individual who honestly satisfies this heart-hunger will hold people in the palm of his hand and "even the undertaker will be sorry when he dies."

The desire for a feeling of importance is one of the chief distinguishing differences between mankind and the animals. To illustrate: When I was a farm boy out in Missouri, my father bred fine Duroc-Jersey hogs and pedigreed white-faced cattle. We used to exhibit our hogs and white-faced cattle at the county fairs and livestock shows throughout the Middle West. We won first prizes by the score. My father pinned his blue ribbons on a sheet of white muslin, and when friends or visitors came to the house, he would get out the long sheet of muslin. He would hold one end and I would hold the other while he exhibited the blue ribbons.

The hogs didn't care about the ribbons they had won. But Father did. These prizes gave him a feeling of importance.

If our ancestors hadn't had this flaming urge for a feeling of importance, civilization would have been impossible. Without it, we should have been just about like the animals.

It was this desire for a feeling of importance that led an uneducated, poverty-stricken grocery clerk to study some law books that he found in the bottom of a barrel of household plunder that he had bought for fifty cents. You have probably heard of this grocery clerk. His name was Lincoln.

It was this desire for a feeling of importance that inspired Dickens to write his immortal novels. This desire inspired Sir Christopher Wren to design his symphonies in stone. This desire made Rockefeller amass millions that he never spent! And this same desire made the richest man in your town build a house far too large for his requirements.

This desire makes you want to wear the latest styles, drive the latest car, and talk about your brilliant children.

It is this desire which lures many boys into becoming gangsters and gunmen. "The average young criminal of today," says E. P. Mulrooney, former Police Commissioner of New York, "is filled with ego, and his first request after arrest is for those lurid newspapers that make him out a hero. The disagreeable prospect of taking a 'hot squat' in the electric chair seems remote, so long as he can gloat over his likeness sharing space with pictures of Babe Ruth, LaGuardia, Einstein, Lindbergh, Toscanini, or Roosevelt."

If you tell me how you get your feeling of importance, I'll tell you what you are. That determines your character. That is the most significant thing about you. For example,

John D. Rockefeller got his feeling of importance by giving money to erect a modern hospital in Peking, China, to care for millions of poor people whom he had never seen and never would see. Dillinger, on the other hand, got his feeling of importance by being a bandit, a bank robber and killer. When the G-men were hunting him, he dashed into a farmhouse up in Minnesota and said, "I'm Dillinger!" He was proud of the fact that he was Public Enemy Number One. "I'm not going to hurt you, but I'm Dillinger!" he said.

Yes, the one significant difference between Dillinger and Rockefeller is how they got their feeling of importance.

History sparkles with amusing examples of famous people struggling for a feeling of importance. Even George Washington wanted to be called "His Mightiness, the President of the United States"; and Columbus pleaded for the title, "Admiral of the Ocean and Viceroy of India." Catherine the Great refused to open letters that were not addressed to "Her Imperial Majesty"; and Mrs. Lincoln, in the White House, turned upon Mrs. Grant like a tigress and shouted, "How dare you be seated in my presence until I invite you!"

Our millionaires helped finance Admiral Byrd's expedition to the Antarctic with the understanding that ranges of icy mountains would be named after them; and Victor Hugo aspired to have nothing less than the city of Paris renamed in his honor. Even Shakespeare, mightiest of the mighty, tried to add luster to his name by procuring a coat of arms for his family.

People sometimes become invalids in order to win sympathy and attention, and get a feeling of importance. For example, take Mrs. McKinley. She got a feeling of importance by forcing her husband, the President of the United States, to neglect important affairs of state while he reclined on the bed beside her for hours at a time, his arms about her, soothing her to sleep. She fed her gnawing desire for attention by insisting that he remain with her while she was having her teeth fixed, and once created a stormy scene when he had to leave her alone with the dentist while he kept an appointment with John Hay.

Mary Roberts Rinehart once told me of a bright, vigorous young woman who became an invalid in order to get a feeling of importance. "One day," said Mrs. Rinehart, "this woman had been obliged to face something, her age perhaps, and the fact that she would never be married. The lonely years were stretching ahead and there was little left for her to anticipate.

"She took to her bed; and for ten years her old mother traveled to the third floor and back, carrying trays, nursing her. Then one day the old mother, weary with service, lay down and died. For some weeks, the invalid languished; then she got up, put on her clothing and resumed living again."

Some authorities declare that people may actually go insane in order to find, in the dreamland of insanity, the feeling of importance that has been denied them in the harsh world of reality. There are more patients suffering from mental diseases in the hospitals in the United States than from all other diseases combined. If you are over fifteen years of age and residing in New York State, the chances are one out of twenty that you will be confined to an asylum for seven years of your life.

What is the cause of insanity?

Nobody can answer such a sweeping question as that, but we know that certain diseases, such as syphilis, break down and destroy the brain cells and result in insanity. In fact, about one-half of all mental diseases can be attributed to such physical causes as brain lesions, alcohol, toxins, and injuries. But the other half—and this is the appalling part of the story—the other half of the people who go insane apparently have nothing organically wrong with their brain cells. In post-mortem examinations, when their brain tissues are studied under the highest-powered microscopes, they are found to be apparently just as healthy as yours and mine.

Why do these people go insane?

I recently put that question to the head physician of one of our most important hospitals for the insane. This doctor, who has received the highest honors and the most coveted

awards for his knowledge of insanity, told me frankly t
he didn't know why people went insane. Nobody know
for sure. But he did say that many people who go insane
find in insanity a feeling of importance that they were
unable to achieve in the world of reality. Then he told
me this story:

"I have a patient right now whose marriage proved to
be a tragedy. She wanted love, sexual gratification, children,
and social prestige; but life blasted all her hopes. Her husband didn't love her. He refused even to eat with her, and
forced her to serve his meals in his room upstairs. She had
no children, no social standing. She went insane; and, in
her imagination, she divorced her husband and resumed
her maiden name. She now believes she has married into
the English aristocracy, and she insists on being called
Lady Smith.

"And as for children, she imagines now that she has a
new child every night. Each time I call on her she says:
'Doctor, I had a baby last night.' "

Life once wrecked all her dream ships on the sharp
rocks of reality; but in the sunny, fantastic isles of insanity, all her barkentines race into port with canvas
billowing and with winds singing through the masts.

Tragic? Oh, I don't know. Her physician said to me:
"If I could stretch out my hand and restore her sanity, I
wouldn't do it. She's much happier as she is."

As a group, insane people are happier than you and I.
Many enjoy being insane. Why shouldn't they? They have
solved their problems. They will write you a check for a
million dollars, or give you a letter of introduction to the
Aga Khan. They have found in a dream world of their
own creation the feeling of importance which they so
deeply desired.

If some people are so hungry for a feeling of importance
that they actually go insane to get it, imagine what miracles
you and I can achieve by giving people honest appreciation
this side of insanity.

There have been, so far as I know, only two people in
history who were paid a salary of a million dollars a year:
Walter Chrysler and Charles Schwab.

Vhy did Andrew Carnegie pay Schwab a million dollars
year or more than three thousand dollars a day? Why?
Because Schwab is a genius? No. Because he knew more
about the manufacture of steel than other people? Non-
sense. Charles Schwab told me himself that he had many
men working for him who knew more about the manufacture of steel than he did.

Schwab says that he was paid this salary largely because of his ability to deal with people. I asked him how
he did it. Here is his secret set down in his own words—
words that ought to be cast in eternal bronze and hung in
every home and school, every shop and office in the land
—words that children ought to memorize instead of
wasting their time memorizing the conjugation of Latin
verbs or the amount of the annual rainfall in Brazil—
words that will all but transform your life and mine if
we will only live them:

*"I consider my ability to arouse enthusiasm among the
men," said Schwab, "the greatest asset I possess, and the
way to develop the best that is in a man is by appreciation
and encouragement.*

*"There is nothing else that so kills the ambitions of a
man as criticisms from his superiors. I never criticize anyone. I believe in giving a man incentive to work. So I am
anxious to praise but loath to find fault. If I like anything,
I am hearty in my approbation and lavish in my praise."*

That is what Schwab does. But what does the average
man do? The exact opposite. If he doesn't like a thing, he
raises the Old Harry; if he does like it, he says nothing.

"In my wide association in life, meeting with many and
great men in various parts of the world," Schwab declared,
"I have yet to find the man, however great or exalted his
station, who did not do better work and put forth greater
effort under a spirit of approval than he would ever do
under a spirit of criticism."

That, he said frankly, was one of the outstanding reasons
for the phenomenal success of Andrew Carnegie. Carnegie
praised his associates publicly as well as privately.

Carnegie wanted to praise his assistants even on his tombstone. He wrote an epitaph for himself which read: "Here lies one who knew how to get around him men who were cleverer than himself."

Sincere appreciation was one of the secrets of Rockefeller's success in handling men. For example, when one of his partners, Edward T. Bedford, pulled a boner and lost the firm a million dollars by a bad buy in South America, John D. might have criticized; but he knew Bedford had done his best—and the incident was closed. So Rockefeller found something to praise; he congratulated Bedford because he had been able to save sixty per cent of the money he had invested. "That's splendid," said Rockefeller. "We don't always do as well as that upstairs."

Ziegfeld, the most spectacular *entrepreneur* who ever dazzled Broadway, gained his reputation by his subtle ability to "glorify the American girl." He repeatedly took some drab little creature that no one ever looked at twice and transformed her on the stage into a glamorous vision of mystery and seduction. Knowing the value of appreciation and confidence, he made women *feel* beautiful by the sheer power of his gallantry and consideration. He was practical: he raised the salary of chorus girls from thirty dollars a week to as high as one hundred and seventy-five. And he was also chivalrous: on opening night at the Follies, he sent a telegram to the stars in the cast, and he deluged every chorus girl in the show with American Beauty roses.

I once succumbed to the fad of fasting and went for six days and nights without eating. It wasn't difficult. I was less hungry at the end of the sixth day than I was at the end of the second. Yet I know, and you know, people who would think they had committed a crime if they let their families or employees go for six days without food; but they will let them go for six days, and six weeks, and sometimes sixty years without giving them the hearty appreciation that they crave almost as much as they crave food.

When Alfred Lunt played the stellar role in *Reunion in*

Vienna, he said, "There is nothing I need so much as nourishment for my self-esteem."

We nourish the bodies of our children and friends and employees; but how seldom do we nourish their self-esteem. We provide them with roast beef and potatoes to build energy; but we neglect to give them kind words of appreciation that would sing in their memories for years like the music of the morning stars.

Some readers are saying right now as they read these lines: "Old stuff! Soft soap! Bear oil! Flattery! I've tried that stuff. It doesn't work—not with intelligent people."

Of course, flattery seldom works with discerning people. It is shallow, selfish, and insincere. It ought to fail and it usually does. True, some people are so hungry, so thirsty, for appreciation that they will swallow anything, just as a starving man will eat grass and fish worms.

Why, for example, were the much-married Mdivani brothers such flaming successes in the matrimonial market? Why were these so-called "Princes" able to marry two beautiful and famous screen stars and a world-famous prima donna and Barbara Hutton with her five-and-ten-cent-store millions? Why? How did they do it?

"The Mdivani charm for women," said Adela Rogers St. John, in an article in the magazine *Liberty*, " . . . has been among the mysteries of the ages to many.

"Pola Negri, a woman of the world, a connoisseur of men, and a great artist, once explained it to me. She said, 'They understand the art of flattery as do no other men I have ever met. And the art of flattery is almost a lost one in this realistic and humorless age. That, I assure you, is the secret of the Mdivani charm for women, I know.' "

Even Queen Victoria was susceptible to flattery. Disraeli confessed that he put it on thick in dealing with the Queen. To use his exact words, he said he "spread it on with a trowel." But Disraeli was one of the most polished, deft, and adroit men who ever ruled the far-flung British Empire. He was a genius in his line. What would work for him wouldn't necessarily work for you and me. In the long run, flattery will do you more harm than good.

Flattery is counterfeit, and like counterfeit money, it will eventually get you into trouble if you try to pass it.

The difference between appreciation and flattery? That is simple. One is sincere and the other insincere. One comes from the heart out; the other from the teeth out. One is unselfish; the other selfish. One is universally admired; the other is universally condemned.

I recently saw a bust of General Obregon in the Chapultepec palace in Mexico City. Below the bust are carved these wise words from General Obregon's philosophy: "Don't be afraid of the enemies who attack you. Be afraid of the friends who flatter you."

No! No! No! I am not suggesting flattery! Far from it. I'm talking about a new way of life. Let me repeat. *I am talking about a new way of life.*

King George V had a set of six maxims displayed on the walls of his study at Buckingham Palace. One of these maxims said: "Teach me neither to proffer nor receive cheap praise." That's all flattery is: cheap praise. I once read a definition of flattery that may be worth repeating: "Flattery is telling the other man precisely what he thinks about himself."

"Use what language you will," said Ralph Waldo Emerson, "you can never say anything but what you are."

If all we had to do was to use flattery, everybody would catch on to it and we should all be experts in human relations.

When we are not engaged in thinking about some definite problem, we usually spend about 95 per cent of our time thinking about ourselves. Now, if we stop thinking about ourselves for awhile and begin to think of the other man's good points, we won't have to resort to flattery so cheap and false that it can be spotted almost before it is out of the mouth.

Emerson said: "Every man I meet is my superior in some way. In that, I learn of him."

If that was true of Emerson, isn't it likely to be a thousand times more true of you and me? Let's cease thinking of our accomplishments, our wants. Let's try to figure out the other man's good points. Then forget flattery.

Give honest, sincere appreciation. Be "hearty in your approbation and lavish in your praise," and people will cherish your words and treasure them and repeat them over a lifetime—repeat them years after you have forgotten them.

CHAPTER THREE

"He Who Can Do This Has the Whole World with Him. He Who Cannot Walks a Lonely Way."

I GO FISHING up in Maine every summer. Personally I am very fond of strawberries and cream; but I find that for some strange reason fish prefer worms. So when I go fishing, I don't think about what I want. I think about what they want. I don't bait the hook with strawberries and cream. Rather, I dangle a worm or a grasshopper in front of the fish and say: "Wouldn't you like to have that?"

Why not use the same common sense when fishing for men?

That is what Lloyd George did. When someone asked him how he managed to stay in power after all the other war-time leaders—Wilson, Orlando, and Clemenceau—had been ousted and forgotten, he replied that if his staying on top might be attributed to any one thing, it was probably to the fact that he had learned it was necessary to bait the hook to suit the fish.

41

about what we want? That is childish. Absurd.
, you are interested in what you want. You are
y interested in it. But no one else is. The rest of us
st like you: we are interested in what we want.

o the only way on earth to influence the other fellow
to talk about what he wants and show him how to get it.

Remember that tomorrow when you are trying to get
somebody to do something. If, for example, you don't
want your son to smoke, don't preach at him, and don't
talk about what you want; but show him that cigarettes
may keep him from making the baseball team or winning
the hundred-yard dash.

This is a good thing to remember regardless of whether
you are dealing with children or calves or chimpanzees.
For example: Ralph Waldo Emerson and his son one day
tried to get a calf into the barn. But they made the common mistake of thinking only of what they wanted: Emerson pushed and his son pulled. But the calf did just what
they did: he thought only of what he wanted; so he stiff-
ened his legs and stubbornly refused to leave the pasture.
The Irish housemaid saw their predicament. She couldn't
write essays and books; but, on this occasion at least, she
had more horse sense, or calf sense, than Emerson had.
She thought of what the calf wanted; so she put her ma-
ternal finger in the calf's mouth, and let the calf suck her
finger as she gently led him into the barn.

Every act you ever performed since the day you were
born is because you wanted something. How about the
time you gave a hundred dollars to the Red Cross? Yes,
that is no exception to the rule. You gave the Red Cross
a hundred dollars because you wanted to lend a helping
hand, because you wanted to do a beautiful, unselfish,
divine act. "Inasmuch as ye have done it unto one of the
least of these my brethren, ye have done it unto me."

If you hadn't wanted that feeling more than you wanted
your hundred dollars, you would not have made the contribution. Of course, you may have made the contribution
because you were ashamed to refuse or because a customer
asked you to do it. But one thing is certain. You made the
contribution because you wanted something.

Professor Harry A. Overstreet in his illuminating book, *Influencing Human Behavior,* says: "Action springs out of what we fundamentally desire . . . and the best piece of advice which can be given to would-be persuaders, whether in business, in the home, in the school, in politics, is: first, arouse in the other person an eager want. He who can do this has the whole world with him. He who cannot walks a lonely way!"

Andrew Carnegie, the poverty-stricken Scotch lad who started to work at two cents an hour and finally gave away three hundred and sixty-five million dollars—he learned early in life that the only way to influence people is to talk in terms of what the other person wants. He attended school only four years, yet he learned how to handle people.

To illustrate: His sister-in-law was worried sick over her two boys. They were at Yale, and they were so busy with their own affairs that they neglected to write home and paid no attention whatever to their mother's frantic letters.

Then Carnegie offered to wager a hundred dollars that he could get an answer by return mail, without even asking for it. Someone called his bet; so he wrote his nephews a chatty letter, mentioning casually in a postscript that he was sending each one a five-dollar bill.

He neglected, however, to enclose the money.

Back came replies by return mail thanking "Dear Uncle Andrew" for his kind note and—you can finish the sentence yourself.

Tomorrow you will want to persuade somebody to do something. Before you speak, pause and ask: "How can I make him *want* to do it?"

That question will stop us from rushing in heedlessly to see people with futile chatter about our desires.

I rent the grand ballroom of a certain New York hotel for twenty nights in each season in order to hold a series of lectures.

At the beginning of one season, I was suddenly informed that I should have to pay almost three times as much rent as formerly. This news reached me after the tickets had been printed and distributed and all announcements had been made.

Naturally, I didn't want to pay the increase, but what was the use of talking to the hotel about what I wanted? They were interested only in what they wanted. So a couple of days later I went in to see the manager.

"I was a bit shocked when I got your letter," I said, "but I don't blame you at all. If I had been in your position, I should probably have written a similar letter myself. Your duty as the manager of this hotel is to make all the profit possible. If you don't do that, you will be fired and you ought to be fired. Now, let's take a piece of paper and write down the advantages and the disadvantages that will accrue to you, if you insist on this increase in rent."

Then I took a letterhead and ran a line through the center and headed one column "Advantages" and the other column "Disadvantages."

I wrote down under the head of "Advantages" these words: "Ballroom free." Then I went on to say: "You will have the advantage of having the ballroom free to rent for dances and conventions. That is a big advantage, for affairs like that will pay you much more than you can get for a series of lectures. If I tie your ballroom up for twenty nights during the course of the season, it is sure to mean a loss of some very profitable business to you.

"Now, let's consider the disadvantages. First, instead of increasing your income from me, you are going to decrease it. In fact, you are going to wipe it out because I cannot pay the rent you are asking. I shall be forced to hold these lectures at some other place.

"There's another disadvantage to you also. These lectures attract crowds of educated and cultured people to your hotel. That is good advertising for you, isn't it? In fact, if you spent $5,000 advertising in the newspapers, you couldn't bring as many people to look at your hotel as I can bring by these lectures. That is worth a lot to a hotel, isn't it?"

As I talked, I wrote these two "disadvantages" under the proper heading, and handed the sheet of paper to the manager, saying: "I wish you would carefully consider both the advantages and disadvantages that are going to accrue to you and then give me your final decision."

I received a letter the next day, informing me that my rent would be increased only 50 per cent instead of 300 per cent.

Mind you, I got this reduction without saying a word about what I wanted. I talked all the time about what the other person wanted, and how he could get it.

Suppose I had done the human, natural thing: suppose I had stormed into his office and said, "What do you mean by raising my rent 300 per cent when you know the tickets have been printed and the announcements made? Three hundred per cent! Ridiculous! Absurd! I won't pay it!"

What would have happened then? An argument would have begun to steam and boil and sputter—and you know how arguments end. Even if I had convinced him that he was wrong, his pride would have made it difficult for him to back down and give in.

Here is one of the best bits of advice ever given about the fine art of human relationships. "If there is any one secret of success," said Henry Ford, "it lies in the ability to get the other person's point of view and see things from his angle as well as from your own."

That is so good, I want to repeat it: "If there is any one secret of success, it lies in the ability to get the other person's point of view and see things from his angle as well as from your own."

That is so simple, so obvious, that anyone ought to see the truth of it at a glance; yet 90 per cent of the people on this earth ignore it 90 per cent of the time.

An example? Look at the letters that come across your desk tomorrow morning, and you will find that most of them violate this high canon of common sense. Take this one, a letter written by the head of the radio department of an advertising agency with offices scattered across the continent. This letter was sent to the managers of local radio stations throughout the country. (I have set down, in parentheses, my reactions to each paragraph.)

"Mr. John Blank,
Blankville,
Indiana.

Dear Mr. Blank:
    The —— company desires to retain its position in advertising agency leadership in the radio field."

> (Who cares what your company desires? I am worried about my own problems. The bank is foreclosing the mortgage on my house, the bugs are destroying the hollyhocks, the stock market tumbled yesterday, I missed the 8:15 this morning, I wasn't invited to the Jones' dance last night, the doctor tells me I have high blood pressure and neuritis and dandruff. And then what happens? I come down to the office this morning worried, open my mail, and here is some little whippersnapper off in New York yapping about what his company wants. Bah! If he only realized what sort of impression his letter makes, he would get out of the advertising busines and start manufacturing sheep dip.)

"This agency's national advertising accounts were the bulwark of the first network. Our subsequent clearances of station time have kept us at the top of agencies year after year."

> (You are big and rich and right at the top, are you? So what? I don't give two whoops in Hades if you are as big as General Motors and General Electric and the General Staff of the U. S. Army all combined. If you had as much sense as a half-witted humming bird, you would realize that I am interested in how big *I* am—not how big you are. All this talk about your enormous success makes me feel small and unimportant.)

"We desire to service our accounts with the last word on radio station information."

(*You* desire! *You* desire. You unmitigated a~~s~~
not interested in what *you* desire or what Mus~
desires, or what Bing Crosby desires. Let me tell ~
once and for all that I am interested in what *I* desi~
—and you haven't said a word about that yet in this
absurd letter of yours.)

*"Will you, therefore, put the —— company on your
preferred list for weekly station information—every single
detail that will be useful to an agency in intelligently
booking time."*

("Preferred list." You have your nerve! You make
me feel insignificant by your big talk about your company—and then you ask me to put you on a "preferred" list, and you don't even say "please" when
you ask it.)

*"A prompt acknowledgment of this letter, giving us
your latest 'doings,' will be mutually helpful."*

(You fool! You mail me a cheap multigraphed letter
—a form letter scattered far and wide like the autumn
leaves; and you have the gall to ask me when I am
worried about the mortgage and the hollyhocks and
my blood pressure, to sit down and dictate a perso~
note acknowledging your multigraphed form l~tt~r—
and you ask me to do it "promptly." Wh~t do you
mean, "promptly"? Don't you know I ~~ just as busy
as you are—or, at least, I like t~ ~~ink I am. And
while we are on that subject, w~~ gave you the lordly
right to order me around~ . . . You say it will be
"mutually helpful." A~ ~~st, at last, you have begun to
see my viewpoint ~ut you are vague about how it
will be to my ~~vantage.)

Very truly yours,
John Blank
Manager Radio Department

. *The enclosed reprint from the* Blankville Journal
e of interest to you and you may want to broadcast it
your station."

(Finally, down here in the postscript, you mention
something that may help me solve one of my problems.
Why didn't you begin your letter with—but what's
the use? Any advertising man who is guilty of per-
petrating such drivel as you have sent me has something wrong with his medulla oblongata. You don't
need a letter giving our latest doings. What you need
is a quart of iodine in your thyroid gland.)

Now if a man who devotes his life to advertising and
who poses as an expert in the art of influencing people to
buy—if he writes a letter like that, what can we expect
from the butcher and baker and carpet-tack maker?

Here is another letter, written by the superintendent of a
large freight terminal to a student of this course, Mr.
Edward Vermylen. What effect did this letter have on the
man to whom it was addressed? Read it and then I'll tell
you.

A. Zerega's Sons, Inc.,
28 Front Street,
Brooklyn, N. Y.

                          Attention: Mr. Edward Vermylen
Gentlemen:
   The operations at our outbound-rail-receiving station are
handicapped because a material percentage of the total
business is delivered us in the late afternoon. This condition results in congestion, overtime on the part of our
forces, delays to trucks, and in some cases delays to
freight. On November 10, we received from your company
a lot of 510 pieces, which reached here at 4:20 P.M.
   We solicit your co-operation toward overcoming the
undesirable effects arising from the late receipt of freight.
May we ask that, on days on which you ship the volume
which was received on the above date, effort be made

either to get the truck here earlier or to deliver <u>t</u>
the freight during the forenoon?

The advantage that would accrue to you under su<u>c</u>
arrangement would be that of more expeditious discha<u>r</u>
of your trucks and the assurance that your business woul<u>d</u>
go forward on the date of its receipt.

Very truly yours,

J—— B——, *Supt.*

After reading this letter, Mr. Vermylen, sales manager for A. Zerega's Sons, Inc., sent it to me with the following comment: "This letter had the reverse effect from that which was intended. The letter begins by describing the Terminal's difficulties, in which we are not interested, generally speaking. Our co-operation is then requested without any thought as to whether it would inconvenience us, and then, finally, in the last paragraph, the fact is mentioned that if we do co-operate it will mean more expeditious discharge of our trucks with the assurance that our freight will go forward on the date of its receipt.

"In other words, that in which we are most interested is mentioned last and the whole effect is one of raising a spirit of antagonism rather than of co-operation."

Let's see if we can't rewrite and improve this letter. Let's not waste any time talking about our problems. As Henry Ford admonishes, let's "get the other person's point of view and see things from his angle as well as from our own."

Here is one way of revising it. It may not be the best way; but isn't it an improvement?

Mr. Edward Vermylen,
c/o A. Zerega's Sons, Inc.,
28 Front Street,
Brooklyn, N. Y.

Dear Mr. Vermylen:

Your company has been one of our good customers for fourteen years. Naturally, we are very grateful for your

…and are eager to give you the speedy, efficient … you deserve. However, we regret to say that it isn't … ole for us to do that when your trucks bring us a … ge shipment late in the afternoon, as they did on November 10. Why? Because many other customers make late afternoon deliveries also. Naturally, that causes congestion. That means your trucks are held up unavoidably at the pier and sometimes even your freight is delayed.

That's bad. Very bad. How can it be avoided? By making your deliveries at the pier in the forenoon when possible. That will enable your trucks to keep moving, your freight will get immediate attention, and our workmen will get home early at night to enjoy a dinner of the delicious macaroni and noodles that you manufacture.

Please don't take this as a complaint, and please don't feel I am assuming to tell you how to run your business. This letter is prompted solely by a desire to serve you more effectively.

Regardless of when your shipments arrive, we shall always cheerfully do all in our power to serve you promptly.

You are busy. Please don't trouble to answer this note.

Yours truly,
J—— B——, *Supt.*

Thousands of salesmen are pounding the pavements today, tired, discouraged, and underpaid. Why? Because they are always thinking only of what they want. They don't realize that neither you nor I want to buy anything. If we did, we would go out and buy it. But both of us are eternally interested in solving our problems. And if a salesman can show us how his services or his merchandise will help us solve our problems, he won't need to sell us. We'll buy. And a customer likes to feel that he is buying—not being sold.

Yet many men spend a lifetime in selling without seeing things from the customer's angle. For example, I live in Forest Hills, a little community of private homes in the center of greater New York. One day as I was rushing to the station, I chanced to meet a real estate operato. had bought and sold property on Long Island for n. years. He knew Forest Hills well so I hurriedly asked h whether or not my stucco house was built with metal lath or hollow tile. He said he didn't know and told me what I already knew: that I could find out by calling the Forest Hills Gardens Association. The following morning, I received a letter from him. Did he give me the information I wanted? He could have gotten it in sixty seconds by a telephone call. But he didn't. He told me again that I could get it by telephoning myself, and then asked me to let him handle my insurance.

He was not interested in helping me. He was interested only in helping himself.

I ought to have given him copies of Vash Young's excellent little books, *The Go-Giver* and *A Fortune to Share*. If he read those books and practiced their philosophy, they would make him a thousand times as much profit as handling my insurance.

Professional men make the same mistake. Several years ago, I walked into the office of a well-known nose-and-throat specialist in Philadelphia. Before he even looked at my tonsils, he asked me what my business was. He wasn't interested in the size of my tonsils. He was interested in the size of my exchequer. His chief concern was not in how much he could help me. His chief concern was in how much he could get out of me. The result was he got nothing. I walked out of his office with contempt for his lack of character.

The world is full of people like that: grabbing, self-seeking. So the rare individual who unselfishly tries to serve others has an enormous advantage. He has little competition. Owen D. Young said: "The man who can put himself in the place of other men, who can understand the workings of their minds, need never worry about what the future has in store for him."

If out of reading this book you get just one thing: an increased tendency to think always in terms of the other person's point of view, and see things from his angle—if

...t that one thing out of this book, it may easily prove
... one of the milestones of your career.

Most men go through college and learn to read Virgil
and master the mysteries of calculus without ever discover-
ing how their own minds function. For instance: I once
gave a course in "Effective Speaking" for the young college
men who were entering the employ of the Carrier Corporation, Newark, New Jersey, the organization that cools office
buildings and air-conditions theatres. One of the men
wanted to persuade the others to play basketball and this
is about what he said: "I want you men to come out and
play basketball. I like to play basketball but the last few
times I have been to the gymnasium there haven't been
enough men there to get up a game. Two or three of us
got to throwing the ball around the other night—and I
got a black eye. I wish you boys would come down
tomorrow night. I want to play basketball."

Did he talk about anything you want? You don't want
to go to a gymnasium that no one else goes to, do you?
You don't care about what he wants. You don't want to
get a black eye.

Could he have shown you how to get the things you
want by using the gymnasium? Surely. More pep. Keener
edge to the appetite. Clearer brain. Fun. Games. Basketball.

To repeat Professor Overstreet's wise advice: "First
arouse in the other person an eager want. He who can do
this has the whole world with him. He who cannot walks a
lonely way."

One of the students in the author's training course was
worried about his little boy. The child was underweight
and refused to eat properly. His parents used the usual
method. They scolded and nagged. "Mother wants you to
eat this and that." "Father wants you to grow up to be a
big man."

Did the boy pay any attention to these pleas? Just about
as much as you pay to one grain of sand on a sandy beach.

No man with a trace of horse sense would expect a
child three years old to react to the viewpoint of a father
thirty years old. Yet that was precisely what that father
had been expecting. It was absurd. He finally saw that.

So he said to himself: "What does that boy v.
I tie up what I want to what he wants?"

It was easy when he started thinking about i.
had a tricycle which he loved to ride up and dc
sidewalk in front of the house in Brooklyn. A few .
down the street lived a "menace," as they say out in Ho.
wood—a bigger boy who would pull the little boy off hr.
tricycle and ride it himself.

Naturally, the little boy would run screaming to his
mother, and she would have to come out and take the
"menace" off the tricycle and put her little boy on again.
This happened almost every day.

What did the little boy want? It didn't take a Sherlock
Holmes to answer that one. His pride, his anger, his desire
for a feeling of importance—all the strongest emotions in
his make-up—goaded him on to get revenge, to smash the
"menace" in the nose. And when his father told him he
could wallop the daylights out of the bigger kid someday
if he would only eat the things his mother wanted him to
eat—when his father promised him that, there was no
longer any problem of dietetics. That boy would have
eaten spinach, sauerkraut, salt mackerel, anything in order
to be big enough to whip the bully who had humiliated
him so often.

After solving that problem, the father tackled another:
the little boy had the unholy habit of wetting his bed.

He slept with his grandmother. In the morning, his
grandmother would wake up and feel the sheet and say:
"Look, Johnny, what you did again last night."

He would say: "No, I didn't do it. You did it."

Scolding, spanking, shaming him, reiterating that mother
didn't want him to do it—none of these things kept the
bed dry. So the parents asked: "How can we make this
boy *want* to stop wetting his bed?"

What were his wants? First, he wanted to wear pajamas
like daddy instead of wearing a nightgown like grandmother. Grandmother was getting fed up with his nocturnal
iniquities so she gladly offered to buy him a pair of
pajamas if he would reform. Second, he wanted a bed of
his own . . . Grandma didn't object.

took him down to Loeser's department store
, winked at the sales girl, and said: "Here is a
eman who would like to do some shopping."

sales girl made him feel important by saying:
ung man, what can I show you?"

He stood a couple of inches taller and said: "I want to
buy a bed for myself."

When he was shown the one his mother wanted him to
buy, she winked at the sales girl and the boy was persuaded
to buy it.

The bed was delivered the next day; and that night
when father came home, the little boy ran to the door
shouting: "Daddy! Daddy! Come upstairs and see *my*
bed that *I* bought."

The father, looking at the bed, obeyed Charles Schwab's
injunction: he was "hearty in his approbation and lavish
in his praise."

"You are not going to wet this bed, are you?" the father
asked.

"Oh, no, no! I am not going to wet this bed." The boy
kept his promise, for his pride was involved. That was *his*
bed. *He* and *he* alone had bought it. And he was wearing
pajamas now like a little man. He wanted to act like a
man. And he did.

Another father, K. T. Dutschmann, a telephone engineer,
a student of this course, couldn't get his three-year-old
daughter to eat breakfast food. The usual scolding, plead-
ing, coaxing methods had all ended in futility. So the
parents asked themselves: "How can we make her *want*
to do it?"

The little girl loved to imitate her mother, to feel big
and grown up; so one morning they put her on a chair and
let her make the breakfast food. At just the psychological
moment, father drifted into the kitchen while she was
stirring the breakfast food and she said: "Oh, look, daddy,
I am making the Maltex this morning."

She ate two helpings of the cereal that morning without
any coaxing because she was interested in it. She had
achieved a feeling of importance; she had found in making
the breakfast food an avenue of self-expression.

William Winter once remarked that "self-e. the dominant necessity of human nature." Why use that same psychology in business? When we brilliant idea, instead of making the other person think ours, why not let him cook and stir the idea himself? will then regard it as his own; he will like it and maybe eat a couple of helpings of it.

Remember: "First arouse in the other person an eager want. He who can do this has the world with him. He who cannot walks a lonely way."

Nine Suggestions on How to Get the Most Out of This Book

1. If you wish to get the most out of this book, there is one indispensable requirement, one essential infinitely more important than any rules or technique. Unless you have this one fundamental requisite a thousand rules on how to study will avail little. And if you do have this cardinal endowment, then you can achieve wonders without reading any suggestions for getting the most out of a book.

What is this magic requirement? Just this: *a deep, driving desire to learn, a vigorous determination to increase your ability to deal with people.*

How can you develop such an urge? By constantly reminding yourself of how important these principles are to you. Picture to yourself how their mastery will aid you in your race for richer social and financial rewards. Say to yourself over and over: "My popularity, my happiness, and my income depend to no small extent upon my skill in dealing with people."

2. Read each chapter rapidly at first to get a bird's-eye view of it. You will probably be tempted then to rush on

to the next one. But don't. Unless you are reading
for entertainment. But if you are reading because you
to increase your skill in human relations, then go b.
and *reread each chapter thoroughly*. In the long run, th.
will mean saving time and getting results.

3. *Stop frequently in your reading to think over what
you are reading*. Ask yourself just how and when you can
apply each suggestion. That kind of reading will aid you
far more than racing ahead like a whippet chasing a rabbit.

4. *Read with a red crayon, pencil, or fountain pen in
your hand; and when you come across a suggestion that
you feel you can use, draw a line beside it*. If it is a four-
star suggestion, then underscore every sentence, or mark it
with "XXXX." Marking and underscoring a book make it
more interesting, and far easier to review rapidly.

5. I know a man who has been office manager for a
large insurance concern for fifteen years. He reads every
month all the insurance contracts his company issues. Yes,
he reads the same contracts over month after month, year
after year. Why? Because experience has taught him that
that is the only way he can keep their provisions clearly
in mind.

I once spent almost two years writing a book on public
speaking; and yet I find I have to keep going back over it
from time to time in order to remember what I wrote in
my own book. The rapidity with which we forget is
astonishing.

*So, if you want to get a real, lasting benefit out of this
book, don't imagine that skimming through it once will
suffice. After reading it thoroughly, you ought to spend a
few hours reviewing it every month. Keep it on your desk
in front of you every day. Glance through it often. Keep
constantly impressing yourself with the rich possibilities
for improvement that still lie in the offing. Remember that
the use of these principles can be made habitual and un-
conscious only by a constant and vigorous campaign of
review and application. There is no other way.*

...rnard Shaw once remarked: "If you teach a man
...ing, he will never learn." Shaw was right. *Learning
.n active process. We learn by doing. So, if you desire to
.aster the principles you are studying in this book, do
something about them. Apply these rules at every opportunity.* If you don't, you will forget them quickly. Only
knowledge that is used sticks in your mind.

You will probably find it difficult to apply these suggestions all the time. I know because I wrote the book,
and yet frequently I find it difficult to apply everything I
have advocated. For example, when you are displeased, it
is much easier to criticize and condemn than it is to try to
understand the other person's viewpoint. It is frequently
easier to find fault than to find praise. It is more natural
to talk about what you want than to talk about what the
other person wants. And so on. So, as you read this book,
remember that you are not merely trying to acquire information. You are attempting to form new habits. Ah yes,
you are attempting a new way of life. That will require
time and persistence and daily application.

*So refer to these pages often. Regard this as a working
handbook on human relations; and whenever you are
confronted with some specific problem—such as handling
a child, winning a wife to your way of thinking, or satisfy-
ing an irritated customer—hesitate about doing the natural
thing, the impulsive thing. That is usually wrong. Instead,
turn to these pages and review the paragraphs you have
underscored. Then try these new ways and watch them
achieve magic for you.*

7. Offer your wife, your son or some business associate
a dime or a dollar every time he or she catches you
violating a certain principle. Make a lively game out of
mastering these rules.

8. The president of an important Wall Street bank
once described, in a talk before one of my classes, a highly
efficient system that he used for self-improvement. This
man had little formal schooling, yet he is now one of the

most important financiers in America, and he c͟
that he owed most of his success to the constant appl͟
of his homemade system. This is what he does. I'll p͟
in his own words as accurately as I can remember.

"For years I have kept an engagement book showing a͟
the appointments I have during the day. My family never
makes any plans for me on Saturday night, for the family
knows that I devote a part of each Saturday evening to the
illuminating process of self-examination and review and
appraisal. After dinner I go off by myself, open my engagement book, and think over all the interviews, discussions,
and meetings that have taken place during the week. I
ask myself:

" 'What mistakes did I make that time?'

" 'What did I do that was right—and in what way could
I have improved my performance?'

" 'What lessons can I learn from that experience?'

"I often find that this weekly review makes me very
unhappy. I am frequently astonished at my own blunders.
Of course, as the years have gone by, these blunders have
become less frequent. Sometimes now I am inclined to pat
myself on the back a little after one of these sessions. This
system of self-analysis, self-education, continued year after
year, has done more for me than any other one thing I have
ever attempted.

"It has helped me improve my ability to make decisions
—and it has aided me enormously in all my contacts with
people. I cannot recommend it too highly."

*Why not use a similar system to check up on your ap-
plication of the principles discussed in this book? If you do,
two things will result.*

*First, you will find yourself engaged in an educational
process that is both intriguing and priceless.*

*Second, you will find that your ability to meet and deal
with people will grow and spread like a green bay tree.*

9. Keep a diary—a diary in which you ought to record
your triumphs in the application of these principles. Be
specific. Give names, dates, results. Keeping such a record

...pire you to greater efforts; and how fascinating these
...s will be when you chance upon them some evening
...s from now!

In Order to Get the Most Out of This Book:

1. Develop a deep, driving desire to master the principles of human relations.
2. Read each chapter twice before going on to the next one.
3. As you read, stop frequently to ask yourself how you can apply each suggestion.
4. Underscore each important idea.
5. Review this book each month.
6. Apply these principles at every opportunity. Use this volume as a working handbook to help you solve your daily problems.
7. Make a lively game out of your learning by offering some friend a dime or a dollar every time he catches you violating one of these principles.
8. Check up each week on the progress you are making. Ask yourself what mistakes you have made, what improvement, what lessons you have learned for the future.
9. Keep a diary in the back of this book showing how and when you have applied these principles.

PART TWO

Six Ways to Make People Like You

CHAPTER ONE

Do This and You'll Be Welcome Anywhere

WHY READ THIS BOOK to find out how to win friends? Why not study the technique of the greatest winner of friends the world has ever known? Who is he? You may meet him tomorrow coming down the street. When you get within ten feet of him, he will begin to wag his tail. If you stop and pat him, he will almost jump out of his skin to show you how much he likes you. And you know that behind this show of affection on his part, there are no ulterior motives: he doesn't want to sell you any real estate, and he doesn't want to marry you.

Did you ever stop to think that a dog is the only animal that doesn't have to work for a living? A hen has to lay eggs; a cow has to give milk; and a canary has to sing. But a dog makes his living by giving you nothing but love.

When I was five years old, my father bought a little yellow-haired pup for fifty cents. He was the light and joy of my childhood. Every afternoon about four-thirty, he would sit in the front yard with his beautiful eyes staring steadfastly at the path, and as soon as he heard my voice or saw me swinging my dinner pail through the buck brush, he was off like a shot, racing breathlessly up the hill to greet me with leaps of joy and barks of sheer ecstasy.

Tippy was my constant companion for five years. Then one tragic night—I shall never forget it—he was killed within ten feet of my head, killed by lightning. Tippy's death was the tragedy of my boyhood.

You never read a book on psychology, Tippy. You didn't need to. You knew by some divine instinct that one can make more friends in two months by becoming genuinely interested in other people than one can in two years by trying to get other people interested in him. Let me repeat that. *You can make more friends in two months by becoming interested in other people than you can in two years by trying to get other people interested in you.*

Yet I know and you know people who blunder through life trying to wigwag other people into becoming interested in them.

Of course, it doesn't work. People are not interested in you. They are not interested in me. They are interested in themselves—morning, noon, and after dinner.

The New York Telephone Company made a detailed study of telephone conversations to find out which word is the most frequently used. You have guessed it: it is the personal pronoun "I." "I." "I." It was used 3,990 times in 500 telephone conversations. "I." "I." "I." "I." "I."

When you see a group photograph that you are in, whose picture do you look for first?

If you think people are interested in you, answer this question: If you died tonight, how many people would come to your funeral?

Why should people be interested in you unless you are first interested in them? Reach for your pencil now and write your reply here:

If we merely try to impress people and get people interested in us, we will never have many true, sincere friends. Friends, real friends, are not made that way.

Napoleon tried it, and in his last meeting with Josephine he said: "Josephine, I have been as fortunate as any man ever was on this earth; and yet, at this hour, you are the only person in the world on whom I can rely." And historians doubt whether he could rely even on her.

The late Alfred Adler, the famous Viennese psychologist, wrote a book entitled *What Life Should Mean to You.* In that book he says: "It is the individual who is not interested in his fellow men who has the greatest difficulties in life and provides the greatest injury to others. It is from among such individuals that all human failures spring."

You may read scores of erudite tomes on psychology without coming across a statement more significant for you and for me. I dislike repetition but Adler's statement is so rich with meaning that I am going to repeat it in italics:

It is the individual who is not interested in his fellow men who has the greatest difficulties in life and provides the greatest injury to others. It is from among such individuals that all human failures spring.

I once took a course in short-story writing at New York University and during that course the editor of *Collier's* talked to our class. He said he could pick up any one of the dozens of stories that drifted across his desk every day, and after reading a few paragraphs he could feel whether or not the author liked people. "If the author doesn't like people," he said, "people won't like his stories."

This hard-boiled editor stopped twice in the course of his talk on fiction writing, and apologized for preaching a sermon. "I am telling you," he said, "the same things your preacher would tell you. But, remember, you have to be interested in people if you want to be a successful writer of stories."

If that is true of writing fiction, you can be sure it is trebly true of dealing with people face to face.

I spent an evening in the dressing room of Howard Thurston the last time be appeared on Broadway—Thurston, the acknowledged dean of magicians. Thurston, the king of legerdemain. For forty years he traveled all over the world, time and again, creating illusions, mystifying audiences, and making people gasp with astonishment. More than sixty million people paid admission to his show, and he made almost two million dollars in profit.

I asked Mr. Thurston to tell me the secret of his success. His schooling certainly had nothing to do with it, for he ran away from home as a small boy, became a hobo, rode in box cars, slept in haystacks, begged his food from door to door, and learned to read by looking out of box cars at signs along the railway.

Did he have a superior knowledge of magic? No, he told me hundreds of books had been written about legerdemain, and scores of people knew as much about it as he did. But he had two things that the others didn't have. First, he had the ability to put his personality across the footlights. He was a master showman. He knew human nature. Everything he did, every gesture, every intonation of his voice, every lifting of an eyebrow had been carefully rehearsed in advance, and his actions were timed to split seconds. But, in addition to that, Thurston had a genuine interest in people. He told me that many magicians would look at the audience and say to themselves, "Well, there is a bunch of suckers out there, a bunch of hicks; I'll fool them all right." But Thurston's method was totally different. He told me every time he entered the stage he said to himself: "I am grateful because these people come to see me. They make it possible for me to make my living in a very agreeable way. I'm going to give them the very best I possibly can."

He declared he never stepped in front of the footlights without first saying to himself over and over: "I love my audience. I love my audience." Ridiculous? Absurd? You are privileged to think about it anything you like. I am merely passing it on to you without comment as a recipe used by one of the most famous magicians of all time.

Madame Schumann-Heink told me much the same thing. In spite of hunger and heartbreak, in spite of a life filled with so much tragedy that she once attempted to kill herself and her babies—in spite of all that, she sang her way up to the top until she became perhaps the most distinguished Wagnerian singer who ever thrilled an audience;

and she, too, confessed that one of the secrets of her success was the fact that she was intensely interested in people.

That, too, was one of the secrets of Theodore Roosevelt's astonishing popularity. Even his servants loved him. His colored valet, James E. Amos, wrote a book about him entitled *Theodore Roosevelt, Hero to His Valet*. In that book, Amos relates this illuminating incident:

> My wife one time asked the President about a bob-white. She had never seen one and he described it to her fully. Some time later, the telephone at our cottage rang. [Amos and his wife lived in a little cottage on the Roosevelt estate at Oyster Bay.] My wife answered it and it was Mr. Roosevelt himself. He had called her, he said, to tell her that there was a bobwhite outside her window and that if she would look out she might see it. Little things like that were so characteristic of him. Whenever he went by our cottage, even though we were out of sight, we would hear him call out: "Oo-oo-oo, Annie!" or "Oo-oo-oo, James!" It was just a friendly greeting as he went by.

How could employees keep from liking a man like that? How could anyone keep from liking him?

Roosevelt called at the White House one day when the President and Mrs. Taft were away. His honest liking for humble people was shown by the fact that he greeted all the old White House servants by name, even the scullery maids.

"When he saw Alice, the kitchen maid," writes Archie Butt, "he asked her if she still made corn bread. Alice told him that she sometimes made it for the servants, but no one ate it upstairs.

" 'They show bad taste,' Roosevelt boomed, 'and I'll tell the President so when I see him.'

"Alice brought a piece to him on a plate, and he went over to the office eating it as he went and greeting gardeners and laborers as he passed. . . .

"He addressed each person just as he was wont to address him in the past. They still whisper about it to each other, and Ike Hoover said with tears in his eyes: 'It is the only happy day we have had in nearly two years, and not one of us would exchange it for a hundred-dollar bill.' "

It was this same intense interest in the problems of other people that made Dr. Charles W. Eliot one of the most successful presidents who ever directed a university—and you will recall that he presided over the destinies of Harvard from four years after the close of the Civil War until five years before the outbreak of World War I. Here is an example of the way Dr. Eliot worked. One day a freshman, L. R. G. Crandon, went to the president's office to borrow fifty dollars from the Students' Loan Fund. The loan was granted. "Then I made my heartfelt thanks and started to leave"—I am quoting Crandon's own words now—"when President Eliot said, 'Pray be seated.' Then he proceeded, to my amazement, to say in effect: 'I am told that you cook and eat in your room. Now I don't think that is at all bad for you if you get the right food and enough of it. When I was in college, I did the same. Did you ever make veal loaf? That, if made from sufficiently mature and sufficiently cooked veal, is one of the best things you could have, because there is no waste. This is the way I used to make it.' He then told me how to pick the veal, how to cook it slowly, with such evaporation that the soup would turn into jelly later, then how to cut it up and press it with one pan inside another and eat it cold."

I have discovered from personal experience that one can win the attention and time and co-operation of even the most sought-after people in America by becoming genuinely interested in them. Let me illustrate:

Years ago I conducted a course in fiction writing at the Brooklyn Institute of Arts and Sciences, and we wanted Kathleen Norris, Fannie Hurst, Ida Tarbell, Albert Payson Terhune, Rupert Hughes, and other distinguished and busy authors to come over to Brooklyn and give us the benefit of their experiences. So we wrote them, saying we admired their work and were deeply interested in getting their advice and learning the secrets of their success.

Each of these letters was signed by about a hundred and

fifty students. We said we realized that they were busy—too busy to prepare a lecture. So we enclosed a list of questions for them to answer about themselves and their methods of work. They liked that. Who wouldn't like it? So they left their homes and traveled over to Brooklyn to give us a helping hand.

By using the same method, I persuaded Leslie M. Shaw, Secretary of the Treasury in Theodore Roosevelt's cabinet, George W. Wickersham, Attorney General in Taft's cabinet, William Jennings Bryan, Franklin D. Roosevelt, and many other prominent men to come and talk to the students of my courses in public speaking.

All of us, be we butcher or baker or the king upon his throne, all of us like people who admire us. Take the German Kaiser, for example. At the close of the World War, he was probably the most savagely and universally despised man on this earth. Even his own nation turned against him when he fled over into Holland to save his neck. The hatred against him was so intense that millions of people would have loved to have torn him limb from limb or burned him at the stake. In the midst of all this forest fire of fury, one little boy wrote the Kaiser a simple, sincere letter glowing with kindliness and admiration. This little boy said that no matter what the others thought, he would always love Wilhelm as his Emperor. The Kaiser was deeply touched by his letter and invited the little boy to come and see him. The boy came, and so did his mother—and the Kaiser married her. That little boy didn't need to read a book on "How to Win Friends and Influence People." He knew how instinctively.

If we want to make friends, let's put ourselves out to do things for other people—things that require time, energy, unselfishness, and thoughtfulness. When the Duke of Windsor was Prince of Wales, he was scheduled to tour South America, and before he started out on that tour he spent months studying Spanish so that he could make public talks in the language of the country; and the South Americans loved him for it.

For years I have made it a point to find out the birthdays of my friends. How? Although I haven't the foggiest

bit of faith in astrology, I begin by asking the other party
whether he believes the date of one's birth has anything to
do with character and disposition. I then ask him to tell
me the month and day of his birth. If he says November 24,
for example, I keep repeating to myself, "November 24,
November 24." The minute his back is turned, I write
down his name and birthday and later transfer it to a
birthday book. At the beginning of each year, I have these
birthday dates scheduled in my calendar pad, so they come
to my attention automatically. When the natal day arrives,
there is my letter or telegram. What a hit it makes! I am
frequently the only person on earth who remembers.

If we want to make friends, let's greet people with
animation and enthusiasm. When somebody calls you on
the telephone, use the same psychology. Say "Hello" in
tones that bespeak how pleased you are to have the person
call. The New York Telephone Company conducts a school
to train its operators to say "Number please" in a tone that
means "Good morning, I am happy to be of service to
you." Let's remember that when we answer the telephone
tomorrow.

Does this philosophy work in business? Does it? I could
cite scores of illustrations; but we have time for only two.

Charles R. Walters, of one of the large banks in New
York City, was assigned to prepare a confidential report
on a certain corporation. He knew of only one man who
possessed the facts he needed so urgently. Mr. Walters
went to see that man, the president of a large industrial
company. As Mr. Walters was ushered into the president's
office, a young woman stuck her head through a door and
told the president that she didn't have any stamps for him
that day.

"I am collecting stamps for my twelve-year-old son,"
the president explained to Mr. Walters.

Mr. Walters stated his mission, and began asking questions. The president was vague, general, nebulous. He
didn't want to talk, and apparently nothing could persuade
him to talk. The interview was brief and barren.

"Frankly, I didn't know what to do," Mr. Walters said as
he related the story to the class. "Then I remembered what

his secretary had said to him—stamps, twelve-year-old son . . . And I also recalled that the foreign department of our bank collected stamps—stamps taken from letters pouring in from every continent washed by the seven seas.

"The next afternoon I called on this man and sent in word that I had some stamps for his boy. Was I ushered in with enthusiasm? Yes, sir. He couldn't have shaken my hand with more enthusiasm if he had been running for Congress. He radiated smiles and good will. 'My George will love this one,' he kept saying as he fondled the stamps. 'And look at this! This is a treasure.'

"We spent half an hour talking stamps and looking at a picture of his boy, and he then devoted more than an hour of his time to giving me every bit of information I wanted —without my even suggesting that he do it. He told me all he knew, and then called in his subordinates and questioned them. He telephoned some of his associates. He loaded me down with facts, figures, reports, and correspondence. In the parlance of newspaper men, I had a scoop."

Here is another illustration:

C. M. Knaphle, Jr., of Philadelphia, had tried for years to sell coal to a large chain-store organization. But the chain-store company continued to purchase its fuel from an out-of-town dealer and continued to haul it right past the door of Knaphle's office. Mr. Knaphle made a speech one night before one of my classes, pouring out his hot wrath upon chain stores, branding them as a curse to the nation.

And still he wondered why he couldn't sell them.

I suggested that he try different tactics. To put it briefly, this is what happened. We staged a debate between members of the course on "Resolved that the spread of the chain store is doing the country more harm than good."

Knaphle, at my suggestion, took the negative side; he agreed to defend the chain stores, and then went straight to an executive of the chain-store organization that he despised and said: "I am not here to try to sell coal. I have come to ask you to do me a favor." He then told about his debate and said, "I have come to you for help because I can't think of anyone else who would be more capable of giving me the facts I want. I am anxious to win this debate; and I'll deeply appreciate whatever help you can give me."

Here is the rest of the story in Mr. Knaphle's own words:

I had asked this man for precisely one minute of his time. It was with that understanding that he consented to see me. After I had stated my case, he motioned me to a chair and talked to me for exactly one hour and forty-seven minutes. He called in another executive who had written a book on chain stores. He wrote to the National Chain Store Association and secured for me a copy of a debate on the subject. He feels that the chain store is rendering a real service to humanity. He is proud of what he is doing for hundreds of communities. His eyes fairly glowed as he talked; and I must confess that he opened my eyes to things I had never even dreamed of. He changed my whole mental attitude.

As I was leaving, he walked with me to the door, put his arm around my shoulder, wished me well in my debate, and asked me to stop in and see him again and let him know how I made out. The last words he said to me were: "Please see me again later in the spring. I should like to place an order with you for coal."

To me that was almost a miracle. Here he was offering to buy coal without my even suggesting it. I had made more headway in two hours by becoming genuinely interested in him and his problems than I could have made in ten years by trying to get him interested in me and my coal.

You didn't discover a new truth, Mr. Knaphle, for a long time ago, a hundred years before Christ was born, a famous old Roman poet, Publius Syrus, remarked: "We are interested in others when they are interested in us."

So if you want people to like you, **Rule 1** is:

Become genuinely interested in other people.

CHAPTER TWO

A Simple Way to Make
a Good Impression

I RECENTLY ATTENDED a dinner party in New York. One of the guests, a woman who had inherited money, was eager to make a pleasing impression on everyone. She had squandered a modest fortune on sables, diamonds, and pearls. But she hadn't done anything whatever about her face. It radiated sourness and selfishness. She didn't realize what every man knows: namely, that the expression a woman wears on her face is far more important than the clothes she wears on her back. (By the way, that is a good line to remember when your wife wants to buy a fur coat.)

Charles Schwab told me his smile had been worth a million dollars. And he was probably understating the truth. For Schwab's personality, his charm, his ability to make people like him were almost wholly responsible for his extraordinary success; and one of the delightful factors in his personality was his captivating smile.

I once spent an afternoon with Maurice Chevalier—and, frankly, I was disappointed. Glum, taciturn, he was sharply different from what I expected—until he smiled. Then it seemed as if the sun had broken through a cloud. If it hadn't been for his smile, Maurice Chevalier would probably still be a cabinet-maker, back in Paris, following the trade of his father and brothers.

Actions speak louder than words, and a smile says, "I like you. You make me happy. I am glad to see you."

That is why dogs make such a hit. They are so glad to see us that they almost jump out of their skins. So, naturally, we are glad to see them.

An insincere grin? No. That doesn't fool anybody. We know it is mechanical and we resent it. I am talking about a real smile, a heart-warming smile, a smile that comes from within, the kind of a smile that will bring a good price in the market place.

The employment manager of a large New York department store told me he would rather hire a sales girl who hadn't finished grade school, if she had a lovely smile, than to hire a doctor of philosophy with a sober face.

The chairman of the board of directors of one of the largest rubber companies in the United States told me that, according to his observations, a man rarely succeeds at anything unless he has fun doing it. This industrial leader doesn't put much faith in the old adage that hard work alone is the magic key that will unlock the door to our desires. "I have known men," he said, "who succeeded because they had a rip-roaring good time conducting their business. Later, I saw those men begin to work at the job. It grew dull. They lost all joy in it, and they failed."

You must have a good time meeting people if you expect them to have a good time meeting you.

I have asked thousands of business men to smile at someone every hour of the day for a week and then come to class and talk about the results. How has it worked? Let's see . . . Here is a letter from William B. Steinhardt, a member of the New York Curb Exchange. His case isn't isolated. In fact, it is typical of hundreds of others.

"I have been married for over eighteen years," writes Mr. Steinhardt, "and in all that time I seldom smiled at my wife or spoke two dozen words to her from the time I got up until I was ready to leave for business. I was one of the worst grouches who ever walked down Broadway.

"Since you asked me to make a talk about my experience with smiles, I thought I would try it for a week. So the next morning, while combing my hair, I looked at my glum mug in the mirror and said to myself, 'Bill, you are going to wipe the scowl off that sour puss of yours today. You are going to smile. And you are going to begin right now.' As I sat down to breakfast, I greeted my wife with a 'Good morning, my dear,' and smiled as I said it.

"You warned me that she might be surprised. Well, you under-estimated her reaction. She was bewildered. She was shocked. I told her that in the future she could expect this as a regular occurrence and I have kept it up every morning now for two months.

"This changed attitude of mine has brought more happiness in our home during these two months than there was during the last year.

"As I leave for my office now, I greet the elevator boy in the apartment house with a 'Good Morning' and a smile. I greet the doorman with a smile. I smile at the cashier in the subway booth when I ask for change. As I stand on the floor on the Curb Exchange, I smile at men who never saw me smile until recently.

"I soon found that everybody was smiling back at me. I treat those who come to me with complaints or grievances in a cheerful manner. I smile as I listen to them and I find that adjustments are accomplished much easier. I find that smiles are bringing me dollars, many dollars every day.

"I make my office with another broker. One of his clerks is a likable young chap, and I was so elated about the results I was getting that I told him recently about my new philosophy of human relations. He then confessed that when I first came to make my office with his firm he thought me a terrible grouch—and only recently changed his mind. He said I was really human when I smiled.

"I have also eliminated criticism from my system. I give appreciation and praise now instead of condemnation. I have stopped talking about what I want. I am now trying to see the other person's viewpoint. And these things have literally revolutionized my life. I am a totally different man, a happier man, a richer man, richer in friendships and happiness—the only things that matter much after all."

Remember this letter was written by a sophisticated, worldly-wise stockbroker who makes his living buying and selling stocks for his own account on the New York Curb Exchange—a business so difficult that 99 out of every 100 who attempt it fail.

You don't feel like smiling? Then what? Two things. First, force yourself to smile. If you are alone, force yourself to whistle or hum a tune or sing. Act as if you were already happy, and that will tend to make you happy. Here is the way the late Professor William James of Harvard put it:

"Action seems to follow feeling, but really action and feeling go together, and by regulating the action, which is under the more direct control of the will, we can indirectly regulate the feeling, which is not.

"Thus the sovereign voluntary path to cheerfulness, if our cheerfulness be lost, is to sit up cheerfully and to act and speak as if cheerfulness were already there. . . ."

Everybody in the world is seeking happiness—and there is one sure way to find it. That is by controlling your thoughts. Happiness doesn't depend on outward conditions. It depends on inner conditions.

It isn't what you have or who you are or where you are or what you are doing that makes you happy or unhappy. It is what you think about it. For example, two people may be in the same place, doing the same thing; both may have about an equal amount of money and prestige—and yet one may be miserable and the other happy. Why? Because of a different mental attitude. I saw just as many happy faces among the Chinese coolies sweating and toiling in the devastating heat of China for seven cents a day as I see on Park Avenue.

"Nothing is good or bad," said Shakespeare, "but thinking makes it so."

Abe Lincoln once remarked that "most folks are about as

happy as they make up their minds to be." He was right. I recently saw a vivid illustration of that truth. I was walking up the stairs of the Long Island station in New York. Directly in front of me thirty or forty crippled boys on canes and crutches were struggling up the stairs. One boy had to be carried up. I was astonished at their laughter and gaiety. I spoke about it to one of the men in charge of the boys. "Oh, yes," he said, "when a boy realizes that he is going to be a cripple for life, he is shocked at first; but, after he gets over the shock, he usually resigns himself to his fate and then becomes happier than normal boys."

I felt like taking my hat off to those boys. They taught me a lesson I hope I shall never forget.

I spent an afternoon with Mary Pickford during the time when she was preparing to get a divorce from Douglas Fairbanks. The world probably imagined at the time that she was distraught and unhappy; but I found her to be one of the most serene and triumphant persons I had ever met. She radiated happiness. Her secret? She has revealed it in a little book of thirty-five pages, a book you might enjoy. Go to your public library and ask for a copy of *Why Not Try God?* by Mary Pickford.

Franklin Bettger, former third baseman for the St. Louis Cardinals, and now one of the most successful insurance men in America, told me that he figured out years ago that a man with a smile is always welcome. So, before entering a man's office, he always pauses for an instant and thinks of the many things he has to be thankful for, works up a great big honest-to-goodness smile, and then enters the room with the smile just vanishing from his face.

This simple technique, he believes, has had much to do with his extraordinary success in selling insurance.

Peruse this bit of sage advice from Elbert Hubbard—but remember, perusing it won't do you any good unless you apply it:

Whenever you go out of doors, draw the chin in, carry the crown of the head high, and fill the lungs to the utmost; drink in the sunshine; greet your friends with a smile, and put soul into every handclasp. Do not fear being misunderstood and do not waste a minute thinking about your enemies. Try to fix firmly in your mind what you would like to do; and then, without veering of direction, you will move straight to the goal. Keep your mind on the great and splendid things you would like to do, and then, as the days go gliding by, you will find yourself unconsciously seizing upon the opportunities that are required for the fulfillment of your desire, just as the coral insect takes from the running tide the element it needs. Picture in your mind the able, earnest, useful person you desire to be, and the thought you hold is hourly transforming you into that particular individual. . . . Thought is supreme. Preserve a right mental attitude— the attitude of courage, frankness, and good cheer. To think rightly is to create. All things come through desire and every sincere prayer is answered. We become like that on which our hearts are fixed. Carry your chin in and the crown of your head high. We are gods in the chrysalis.

The ancient Chinese are a wise lot—wise in the ways of the world; and they have a proverb that you and I ought to cut out and paste inside our hats. It goes like this: "A man without a smiling face must not open a shop."

And speaking of shops, Frank Irving Fletcher, in one of his advertisements for Oppenheim, Collins & Co., gave us this bit of homely philosophy.

The Value of a Smile at Christmas

It costs nothing, but creates much.

It enriches those who receive, without impoverishing those who give.

It happens in a flash and the memory of it sometimes lasts forever.

None are so rich they can get along without it, and none so poor but are richer for its benefits.

It creates happiness in the home, fosters good will in a business, and is the countersign of friends.

It is rest to the weary, daylight to the discouraged, sunshine to the sad, and Nature's best antidote for trouble.

Yet it cannot be bought, begged, borrowed, or stolen, for it is something that is no earthly good to anybody till it is given away!

And if in the last-minute rush of Christmas buying some of our salespeople should be too tired to give you a smile, may we ask you to leave one of yours?

For nobody needs a smile so much as those who have none left to give!

So if you want people to like you, **Rule 2** is:

Smile.

CHAPTER THREE

If You Don't Do This,
You are Headed for Trouble

BACK IN 1898, a tragic thing happened in Rockland County, New York. A child had died and on this particular day the neighbors were preparing to go to the funeral. Jim Farley went out to the barn to hitch up his horse. The ground was covered with snow, the air was cold and snappy; the horse hadn't been exercised for days; and as he was led out to the watering trough, he wheeled playfully, kicked both his heels high into the air, and killed Jim Farley. So the little village of Stony Point had two funerals that week instead of one.

Jim Farley left behind him a widow and three boys, and a few hundred dollars in insurance.

His oldest boy, Jim, was ten, and he went to work in a brickyard, wheeling sand and pouring it into the molds and turning the brick on edge to be dried by the sun. This boy Jim never had a chance to get much education. But with his Irish geniality, he had a flair for making people like him, so he went into politics and, as the years went by, he developed an uncanny ability for remembering people's names.

He never saw the inside of a high school; but before he was forty-six years of age, four colleges had honored him with degrees, he had become chairman of the Democratic National Committee, and Postmaster General of the United States.

I once interviewed Jim Farley and asked him the secret of his success. He said, "Hard work," and I said, "Don't be funny."

He then asked me what I thought was the reason for his success. I replied: "I understand you can call ten thousand people by their first names."

"No. You are wrong," he said. "I can call fifty thousand people by their first names."

Make no mistake about it. That ability helped Mr. Farley put Franklin D. Roosevelt in the White House.

During the years that Jim Farley traveled as a salesman for a gypsum concern, and during the years that he held office as town clerk in Stony Point, he built up a system for remembering names.

In the beginning, it was a very simple one. Whenever he met a new acquaintance, he found out his complete name, the size of his family, the nature of his business, and the color of his political opinions. He got all these facts well in mind as part of the picture. and the next time he met that man, even if it was a year later, he was able to slap him on the back, inquire after the wife and kids, and ask him about the hollyhocks in the backyard. No wonder he developed a following!

For months before Roosevelt's campaign for President began, Jim Farley wrote hundreds of letters a day to people all over the western and northwestern states. Then he hopped onto a train and in nineteen days covered twenty states and twelve thousand miles, traveling by buggy, train, automobile. and skiff. He would drop into town, meet his people at lunch or breakfast, tea or dinner, and give them a "heart-to-heart talk." Then he'd dash off again on another leg of his journey.

As soon as he arrived back East, he wrote to one man in

each town he had visited, asking for a list of all the guests to whom he had talked. The final list contained thousands and thousands of names; yet each person on that list was paid the subtle flattery of getting a personal letter from James Farley. These letters began "Dear Bill" or "Dear Joe" and they were always signed "Jim."

Jim Farley discovered early in life that the average man is more interested in his own name than he is in all the other names on earth put together. Remember that name and call it easily, and you have paid him a subtle and very effective compliment. But forget it or misspell it—and you have placed yourself at a sharp disadvantage. For example, I once organized a public speaking course in Paris and sent multigraphed letters to all the American residents in the city. French typists with apparently little knowledge of English filled in the names and naturally they made blunders. One man, the manager of a large American bank in Paris, wrote me a scathing rebuke because his name had been misspelled.

What was the reason for Andrew Carnegie's success?

He was called the Steel King; yet he himself knew little about the manufacture of steel. He had hundreds of men working for him who knew far more about steel than he did.

But he knew how to handle men—and that is what made him rich. Early in life, he showed a flair for organization, a genius for leadership. By the time he was ten, he too had discovered the astonishing importance people place on their own names. And he used that discovery to win co-operation. To illustrate: When he was a boy back in Scotland, he got hold of a rabbit, a mother rabbit. Presto! He soon had a whole nest of little rabbits—and nothing to feed them. But he had a brilliant idea. He told the boys in the neighborhood that if they would go out and pull enough clover and dandelions to feed the rabbits, he would name the bunnies in their honor.

The plan worked like magic; and Carnegie never forgot it.

Years later, he made millions by using that same psychology in business. For example, he wanted to sell steel rails to the Pennsylvania Railroad. J. Edgar Thomson was the president of the Pennsylvania Railroad then. So, Andrew Carnegie built a huge steel mill in Pittsburgh and called it the "Edgar Thomson Steel Works."

Here is a riddle. See if you can guess it. When the Pennsylvania Railroad needed steel rails, where do you suppose J. Edgar Thomson bought them? . . . From Sears, Roebuck? No. No. You're wrong. Guess again.

When Carnegie and George Pullman were battling each other for supremacy in the sleeping-car business, the Steel King again remembered the lesson of the rabbits.

The Central Transportation Company, which Andrew Carnegie controlled, was fighting with the company Pullman owned. Both were struggling to get the sleeping-car business of the Union Pacific Railroad, bucking each other, slashing prices, and destroying all chance of profit. Both Carnegie and Pullman had gone to New York to see the board of directors of the Union Pacific. Meeting one evening in the St. Nicholas Hotel, Carnegie said: "Good evening, Mr. Pullman, aren't we making a couple of fools of ourselves?"

"What do you mean?" Pullman demanded.

Then Carnegie expressed what he had on his mind—a merger of their two interests. He pictured in glowing terms the mutual advantage of working with, instead of against, each other. Pullman listened attentively, but he was not wholly convinced. Finally he asked, "What would you call the new company?" and Carnegie replied promptly: "Why the Pullman Palace Car Company, of course."

Pullman's face brightened. "Come into my room," he said. "Let's talk it over." That talk made industrial history.

This policy of Andrew Carnegie's of remembering and honoring the names of his friends and business associates was one of the secrets of his leadership. He was proud of the fact that he could call many of his laborers by their first names; and he boasted that while he was personally in charge, no strike ever disturbed his flaming steel mills.

Paderewski, on the other hand, made his colored Pullman chef feel important by always addressing him as "Mr. Copper." On fifteen different occasions, Paderewski toured America, playing to wildly enthusiastic audiences from coast to coast; and on each occasion he traveled in a private car and the same chef had a midnight meal ready for him after the concert. Never in all those years did Paderewski ever call him "George" after the American manner. With his old-world formality, Paderewski always spoke to him as "Mr. Copper," and Mr. Copper loved it.

Men are so proud of their names that they strive to perpetuate them at any cost. Even blustering, hard-boiled old P. T. Barnum, disappointed because he had no sons to carry on his name, offered his grandson, C. H. Seeley, twenty-five thousand dollars if he would call himself "Barnum" Seeley.

Two hundred years ago, rich men used to pay authors to dedicate their books to them.

Libraries and museums owe their richest collections to men who cannot bear to think that their names might perish from the memory of the race. The New York Public Library has its Astor and Lenox collections. The Metropolitan Museum perpetuates the names of Benjamin Altman and J. P. Morgan. And nearly every church is beautified by stained-glass windows commemorating the names of the donors.

Most people don't remember names for the simple reason that they don't take the time and energy necessary to concentrate and repeat and fix names indelibly in their minds. They make excuses for themselves; they are too busy.

But they are probably no busier than Franklin D. Roosevelt, and he took time to remember and recall even the names of mechanics with whom he came in contact.

To illustrate: The Chrysler organization built a special car for Mr. Roosevelt. W. F. Chamberlain and a mechanic delivered it to the White House. I have in front of me a letter from Mr. Chamberlain relating his experiences. "I taught President Roosevelt how to handle a car with a lot of unusual gadgets; but he taught me a lot about the fine art of handling people."

"When I called at the White House," Mr. Chamberlain

writes, "the President was extremely pleasant and cheerful. He called me by name, made me feel very comfortable, and particularly impressed me with the fact that he was *vitally interested* in the things I had to show him and tell him. The car was so designed that it could be operated entirely by hand. A crowd gathered around to look at the car; and he remarked: 'I think it is marvelous. All you have to do is to touch a button and it moves away and you can drive it without effort. I think it is grand—I don't know what makes it go. I'd love to have the time to tear it down and see how it works.'

"When Roosevelt's friends and associates admired the machine, he said in their presence: 'Mr. Chamberlain, I certainly appreciate all the time and effort you have spent in developing this car. It is a mighty fine job.' He admired the radiator, the special rear-vision mirror and clock, the special spotlight, the kind of upholstery, the sitting position of the driver's seat, the special suitcases in the trunk with his monogram on each suitcase. In other words, he took notice of every detail to which he knew I had given considerable thought. He made a point of bringing these various pieces of equipment to the attention of Mrs. Roosevelt, Miss Perkins, the Secretary of Labor, and his secretary. He even brought the old colored porter into the picture by saying, 'George, you want to take particularly good care of the suitcases.'

"When the driving lesson was finished, the President turned to me and said: 'Well, Mr. Chamberlain, I have been keeping the Federal Reserve Board waiting thirty minutes. I guess I had better get back to work.'

"I took a mechanic with me down to the White House. He was introduced to Roosevelt when he arrived. He didn't talk to the President and Roosevelt heard his name only once. He was a shy chap, and he kept in the background. But before leaving us, the President looked for the mechanic, shook his hand, called him by name, and thanked him for coming down to Washington. And there was nothing perfunctory about his thanks. He meant what he said. I could feel that.

"A few days after returning to New York, I got an autographed photograph of President Roosevelt and a little note of thanks again expressing his appreciation for my assistance. How he found time to do it is a mystery to me."

Franklin D. Roosevelt knew that one of the simplest, most obvious, and most important ways of gaining good will is by remembering names and making people feel important—yet how many of us do it?

Half the time we are introduced to a stranger, chat a few minutes, and can't even remember his name when we say good-by.

One of the first lessons a politician learns is this: "To recall a voter's name is statesmanship. To forget it is oblivion."

And the ability to remember names is almost as important in business and social contacts as it is in politics.

Napoleon the Third, Emperor of France and nephew of the great Napoleon, boasted that in spite of all his royal duties he could remember the name of every person he met.

His technique? Simple. If he didn't hear the name distinctly, he said, "So sorry. I didn't get the name clearly." Then, if it was an unusual name, he would say, "How is it spelled?"

During the conversation, he took the trouble to repeat the name several times, and tried to associate it in his mind with the man's features, expression, and general appearance.

If the man were someone of importance, Napoleon went to even further pains. As soon as His Royal Highness was alone, he wrote the man's name down on a piece of paper, looked at it, concentrated on it, fixed it securely in his mind, and then tore up the paper. In this way, he gained an eye impression of the name as well as an ear impression.

All this takes time, but "good manners," said Emerson, "are made up of petty sacrifices."

So if you want people to like you, **Rule 3** is:

Remember that a man's name is to him the sweetest and most important sound in any language.

CHAPTER FOUR

An Easy Way to Become a Good Conversationalist

I WAS RECENTLY INVITED to a bridge party. Personally, I don't play bridge—and there was a blonde there who didn't play bridge either. She had discovered that I had once been Lowell Thomas' manager before he went on the radio, that I had traveled in Europe a great deal while helping him prepare the illustrated travel talks he was then delivering. So she said: "Oh, Mr. Carnegie, I do want you to tell me about all the wonderful places you have visited and the sights you have seen."

As we sat down on the sofa, she remarked that she and her husband had recently returned from a trip to Africa. "Africa!" I exclaimed. "How interesting! I always wanted to see Africa, but I never got there except for a twenty-four-hour stay once in Algiers. Tell me, did you visit the big-game country? Yes? How fortunate! I envy you! Do tell me about Africa."

That was good for forty-five minutes. She never again asked me where I had been or what I had seen. She didn't want to hear me talk about my travels. All she wanted was an interested listener, so she could expand her ego and tell about where she had been.

Was she unusual? No. Many people are like that.

For example, I recently met a distinguished botanist at a dinner party given by J. W. Greenberg, the New York book publisher. I had never talked to a botanist before, and I found him fascinating. I literally sat on the edge of my chair and listened while he spoke of hashish and Luther Burbank and indoor gardens and told me astonishing facts about the humble potato. I have a small indoor garden of my own—and he was good enough to tell me how to solve some of my problems.

As I said, we were at a dinner party. There must have been a dozen other guests there; but I violated all the canons of courtesy, ignored everyone else, and talked for hours to the botanist.

Midnight came. I said good night to everyone and departed. The botanist then turned to our host and paid me several flattering compliments. I was "most stimulating." I was this and I was that; and he ended up by saying I was a "most interesting conversationalist."

An interesting conversationalist? I? Why, I had said hardly anything at all. I couldn't have said anything if I had wanted to without changing the subject, for I don't know any more about botany than I know about the anatomy of a penguin. But I had done this: I had listened intently. I had listened because I was genuinely interested. And he felt it. Naturally that pleased him. That kind of listening is one of the highest compliments we can pay to anyone. "Few human beings," wrote Jack Woodford in *Strangers in Love,* "few human beings are proof against the implied flattery of rapt attention." I went even farther than giving him rapt attention. I was "hearty in my approbation and lavish in my praise."

I told him I had been immensely entertained and instructed—and I had. I told him I wished that I had his knowledge—and I do. I told him that I should love to wander the fields with him—and I should. I told him I must see him again—and I must.

And so I had him thinking of me as a good conversationalist when, in reality, I had been merely a good listener and encouraged him to talk.

What is the secret, the mystery, of a successful business interview? Well, according to that genial scholar Charles W. Eliot, "there is no mystery about successful business intercourse. . . . Exclusive attention to the person who is speaking to you is very important. Nothing else is so flattering as that."

Self-evident, isn't it? You don't have to study for four years in Harvard to discover that. Yet I know and you know merchants who will rent expensive space, buy their goods economically, dress their windows appealingly, spend hundreds of dollars in advertising, and then hire clerks who haven't the sense to be good listeners—clerks who interrupt customers, contradict them, irritate them, and all but drive them from the store.

Take, for example, the experience of J. C. Wootton. He related this story in one of my classes: He bought a suit in a department store in the enterprising city of Newark, New Jersey. The suit proved to be disappointing; the dye of the coat rubbed off and darkened the collar of his shirt.

Taking the suit back to the store, he found the salesman he had dealt with and told his story. Did I say he "told" his story? Sorry, that is an exaggeration. He *attempted* to tell his story. But he couldn't. He was interrupted.

"We've sold thousands of those suits," the salesman retorted, "and this is the first complaint we have ever had."

That was what his words said; and his tones were even worse. His belligerent tones said: "You are lying. Think you are going to put something over on us, don't you? Well, I'll show you a thing or two."

In the heat of this argument, a second salesman pitched in. "All dark suits rub a little at first," he said. "That can't be helped. Not in suits at that price. It's in the dye."

"By this time, I was fairly sizzling," Mr. Wootton remarked as he told his story. "The first salesman questioned my honesty. The second one intimated that I had purchased a second-rate article. I boiled. I was on the point of telling them to take their suit and go to hell, when suddenly the head of the department strolled by. He knew his business. He changed my attitude completely. He turned an angry man into a satisfied customer. How did he do it? By three things:

"First, *he listened to my story from beginning to end without saying a word.*

"Second, when I had finished and the salesmen again started to air their views, he argued with them from *my point of view.* Not only did he point out that my collar obviously was stained from the suit, but he also insisted that nothing should be sold from that store that did not give complete satisfaction.

"Third, he admitted he didn't know the cause of the trouble and said to me very simply, 'What would you like me to do with the suit? I'll do anything you say.'

"Only a few minutes before I had been ready to tell them to keep their confounded suit. But now I answered, 'I want only your advice. I want to know whether the condition is temporary, and if anything can be done about it.'

"He suggested that I try the suit for another week. 'If it isn't satisfactory then,' he promised, 'bring it in and we'll give you one that is. We are so sorry to have caused you this inconvenience.'

"I walked out of the store satisfied; the suit was all right at the end of the week; and my confidence in that department store was completely restored."

Small wonder that manager was head of his department; and, as for his subordinates, they will remain—I was about to say they would remain clerks all their lives. No, they will probably be demoted to the wrapping department, where they never will come in contact with customers.

The chronic kicker, even the most violent critic, will frequently soften and be subdued in the presence of a patient, sympathetic listener—a listener who will be silent while the irate fault-finder dilates like a king cobra and spews the poison out of his system. To illustrate: The New York Telephone Company discovered a few years ago that it had to deal with one of the most vicious customers who ever cursed a "hello girl." And he did curse. He raved. He threatened to tear the phone out by its roots. He refused to pay certain charges which he declared were false. He wrote letters to the newspapers. He filed innumerable complaints with the Public Service Commission and he started several suits against the telephone company.

At last, one of the company's most skillful "trouble shooters" was sent to interview this stormy petrel. This "trouble shooter" listened and let the cantankerous old boy enjoy himself by pouring out his tirade. The telephone man listened and said "yes" and sympathized with his grievance.

"He raved on and I listened for nearly three hours," the "trouble shooter" said as he related his experiences before one of the author's classes. "Then I went back and listened some more. I interviewed him four times, and before the fourth visit was over I had become a charter member of an organization he was starting. He called it the 'Telephone Subscribers' Protective Association.' I am still a member of this organization, and, so far as I know, I'm the only member in the world today besides Mr. ——.

"I listened and sympathized with him on every point that he made during these interviews. He had never had a telephone man talk to him that way before, and he became almost friendly. The point on which I went to see him was not even mentioned on the first visit, nor was it mentioned on the second or third, but upon the fourth interview I closed the case completely, had all bills paid in full, and for the first time in the history of his difficulties with the Telephone Company he withdrew his complaints to the Commission."

Doubtless Mr. —— considered himself to be a holy crusader, defending the public rights against callous exploitation. But in reality, what he wanted was a feeling of importance. He got this feeling of importance at first by kicking and complaining. But as soon as he got his feeling of importance from a representative of the company, his imagined grievances vanished into thin air.

One morning, years ago, an angry customer stormed into

the office of Julian F. Detmer, founder of the Detmer Woolen Company, which later became the world's largest distributors of woolens to the tailoring trade.

"This man owed us fifteen dollars," Mr. Detmer explained to me. "The customer denied it, but we knew he was wrong. So our credit department had insisted that he pay. After getting a number of letters from our credit men, he packed his grip, made a trip to Chicago, and hurried into my office to inform me not only that he was not going to pay that bill, but that he was never going to buy another dollar's worth of goods from the Detmer Woolen Company.

"I listened patiently to all he had to say. I was tempted to interrupt, but I realized that would be bad policy. So I let him talk himself out. When he finally simmered down and got in a receptive mood, I said quietly: 'I want to thank you for coming to Chicago to tell me about this. You have done me a great favor, for if our credit department has annoyed you, it may annoy other good customers, and that would be just too bad. Believe me, I am far more eager to hear this than you are to tell it.'

"That was the last thing in the world he expected me to say. I think he was a trifle disappointed, because he had come to Chicago to tell me a thing or two, but here I was thanking him instead of scrapping with him. I assured him we would wipe the fifteen-dollar charge off the books and forget it, because he was a very careful man with only one account to look after, while our clerks had to look after thousands. Therefore he was less likely to be wrong than we were.

"I told him that I understood exactly how he felt and that, if I were in his shoes, I should undoubtedly feel precisely as he did. Since he wasn't going to buy from us any more, I recommended some other woolen houses.

"In the past, we had usually lunched together when he came to Chicago, so I invited him to have lunch with me this day. He accepted reluctantly, but when we came back to the office he placed a larger order than ever before. He returned home in a softened mood and, wanting to be just as fair with us as we had been with him, looked over his bills, found one that had been mislaid, and sent us a check for fifteen dollars, with his apologies.

"Later, when his wife presented him with a baby boy, he gave his son the middle name of Detmer and he remained a friend and customer of the house until his death twenty-two years afterwards."

Years ago, a poor Dutch immigrant boy was washing the windows of a bakery shop after school for fifty cents a week, and his people were so poor that he used to go out in the street with a basket every day and collect stray bits of coal that had fallen in the gutter where the coal wagons had delivered fuel. That boy, Edward Bok, never got more than six years' schooling in his life; yet eventually he made himself one of the most successful magazine editors in the history of American journalism. How did he do it? That is a long story, but how he got his start can be told briefly. He got his start by using the principles advocated in this chapter.

He left school when he was thirteen and became an office boy for the Western Union at six dollars and twenty-five cents a week; but he didn't for one moment give up the idea of an education. Instead, he started to educate himself. He saved his car-fares and went without lunch until he had enough money to buy an encyclopedia of American biography—and then he did an unheard-of thing. He read the lives of famous men and wrote them asking for additional information about their childhoods. He was a good listener. He encouraged famous people to talk about themselves. He wrote General James A. Garfield, who was then running for President, and asked if it was true that he was once a tow boy on a canal; and Garfield replied. He wrote General Grant asking about a certain battle; and Grant drew a map for him and invited this fourteen-year-old boy to dinner and spent the evening talking to him.

He wrote Emerson and encouraged Emerson to talk about himself. This Western Union messenger boy was soon corresponding with many of the most famous people in the nation: Emerson, Phillips Brooks, Oliver Wendell Holmes, Longfellow, Mrs. Abraham Lincoln, Louisa May Alcott, General Sherman, and Jefferson Davis.

He not only corresponded with these distinguished people but as soon as he got a vacation he visited many of them as a welcome guest in their homes. This experience imbued him with a confidence that was invaluable. These men and women fired him with a vision and ambition that revolutionized his life. And, all this, let me repeat, was made possible solely by the application of the principles we are discussing here.

Isaac F. Marcosson, who is probably the world's champion interviewer of celebrities, declared that many people fail to make a favorable impression because they don't listen attentively. "They have been so much concerned with what they are going to say next that they do not keep their ears open. . . . Big men have told me that they prefer good listeners to good talkers, but the ability to listen seems rarer than almost any other good trait."

And not only big men crave a good listener, but ordinary folk do too. As the *Reader's Digest* once said: "Many persons call a doctor when all they want is an audience."

During the darkest hours of the Civil War, Lincoln wrote to an old friend out in Springfield, Illinois, asking him to come to Washington. Lincoln said he had some problems he wanted to discuss with him. The old neighbor called at the White House, and Lincoln talked to him for hours about the advisability of issuing a proclamation freeing the slaves. Lincoln went over all the arguments for and against such a move, and then read letters and newspaper articles, some denouncing him for not freeing the slaves and others denouncing him for fear he was going to free them. After talking for hours, Lincoln shook hands with his old neighbor, said good night, and sent him back to Illinois without even asking for his opinion. Lincoln had done all the talking himself. That seemed to clarify his mind. "He seemed to feel easier after the talk," the old friend said. Lincoln hadn't wanted advice. He had wanted merely a friendly, sympathetic listener to whom he could unburden himself. That's what we all want when we are in trouble. That is frequently all the irritated customer wants, and the dissatisfied employee or the hurt friend.

If you want to know how to make people shun you and laugh at you behind your back and even despise you, here is the recipe: Never listen to anyone for long. Talk incessantly about yourself. If you have an idea while the other fellow is talking, don't wait for him to finish. He isn't as smart as you. Why waste your time listening to his idle chatter? Bust right in and interrupt him in the middle of a sentence.

Do you know people like that? I do, unfortunately; and the astonishing part of it is that some of them have their names in the social register.

Bores, that is all they are—bores intoxicated with their own egos, drunk with a sense of their own importance.

The man who talks only of himself, thinks only of himself. And "the man who thinks only of himself," says Dr. Nicholas Murray Butler, president of Columbia University, "is hopelessly uneducated." "He is not educated," says Dr. Butler, "no matter how instructed he may be."

So if you aspire to be a good conversationalist, be an attentive listener. As Mrs. Charles Northam Lee puts it: "To be interesting, be interested." Ask questions that the other man will enjoy answering. Encourage him to talk about himself and his accomplishments.

Remember that the man you are talking to is a hundred times more interested in himself and his wants and his problems than he is in you and your problems. His toothache means more to him than a famine in China that kills a million people. A boil on his neck interests him more than forty earthquakes in Africa. Think of that the next time you start a conversation.

So if you want people to like you, **Rule 4** is:

Be a good listener. Encourage others to talk about themselves.

CHAPTER FIVE

How to Interest People

EVERYONE WHO VISITED Theodore Roosevelt at Oyster Bay was astonished at the range and diversity of his knowledge. "Whether it was a cowboy or a Rough Rider, a New York politician or a diplomat," wrote Gamaliel Bradford, "Roosevelt knew what to say to him." And how was it done? The answer was simple. Whenever Roosevelt expected a visitor, he sat up late the night before reading up on the subject in which he knew his guest was particularly interested.

For Roosevelt knew, as all leaders know, that the *royal road to a man's heart is to talk to him about the things he treasures most.*

The genial William Lyon Phelps, erstwhile professor of literature at Yale, learned this lesson early in life.

"When I was eight years old and was spending a weekend visiting my Aunt Libby Linsley at her home in Stratford on the Housatonic," writes William Lyon Phelps in his essay on *Human Nature,* "a middle-aged man called one evening, and after a polite skirmish with my aunt, he devoted his attention to me. At that time, I happened to be excited about boats, and the visitor discussed the subject in a way that seemed to me particularly interesting. After he left, I spoke of him with enthusiasm. What a man! And how tremendously interested in boats! My aunt informed me he was a New York lawyer; that he cared nothing whatever about boats—took not the slightest interest in the subject. 'But why then did he talk all the time about boats?'

" *'Because he is a gentleman. He saw you were interested in boats, and he talked about the things he knew would interest and please you. He made himself agreeable.' "*

And William Lyon Phelps adds: "I never forgot my aunt's remark."

As I write this chapter, I have before me a letter from Edward L. Chalif, a man active in Boy Scout work.

"One day I found I needed a favor," writes Mr. Chalif. "A big Scout jamboree was coming off in Europe, and I wanted the president of one of the largest corporations in America to pay the expenses of one of my boys for the trip.

"Fortunately, just before I went to see this man, I heard that he had drawn a check for a million dollars, and that after it was cancelled, he had had it framed.

"So the first thing I did when I entered his office was to ask to see that check. A check for a million dollars! I told him I never knew that anybody had ever written such a check, and that I wanted to tell my boys that I had actually seen a check for a million dollars. He gladly showed it to me; I admired it and asked him to tell me all about how it happened to be drawn."

You notice, don't you, that Mr. Chalif didn't begin by talking about the Boy Scouts, or the jamboree in Europe, or what it was *he* wanted? He talked in terms of what interested the other man. Here's the result:

"Presently the man I was interviewing said: 'Oh, by the way, what was it you wanted to see me about?' So I told him.

"To my vast surprise," Mr. Chalif continues, "he not only granted immediately what I asked for, but much more. I had asked him to send only one boy to Europe, but he sent five boys and myself, gave me a letter of credit for a thousand dollars and told us to stay in Europe for seven weeks. He also gave me letters of introduction to his branch presidents, putting them at our service; and he himself met us in Paris and showed us the town. Since then, he has given jobs to some of the boys whose parents were in want; and he is still active in our group.

"Yet I know if I hadn't found out what he was interested in, and got him warmed up first, I wouldn't have found him one-tenth as easy to approach."

Is this a valuable technique to use in business? Is it? Let's see. Take Henry G. Duvernoy, of Duvernoy & Sons, one of the highest-class baking firms in New York.

Mr. Duvernoy had been trying to sell bread to a certain New York hotel. He had called on the manager every week for four years. He went to the same social affairs the manager attended. He even took rooms in the hotel and lived there in order to get the business. But he failed.

"Then," said Mr. Duvernoy, "after studying human relations, I resolved to change my tactics. I decided to find out what interested this man—what caught his enthusiasm.

"I discovered he belonged to a society of hotel men called the Hotel Greeters of America. He not only belonged, but his bubbling enthusiasm had made him president of the organization, and president of the International Greeters. No matter where its conventions were held, he would be there even if he had to fly over mountains or cross deserts or seas.

"So when I saw him the next day, I began talking about the Greeters. What a response I got. What a response! He talked to me for half an hour about the Greeters, his tones vibrant with enthusiasm. I could plainly see that this society was his hobby, the passion of his life. Before I left his office, he 'sold' me a membership in his organization.

"In the meantime, I had said nothing about bread. But a few days later, the steward of his hotel phoned me to come over with samples and prices.

" 'I don't know what you did to the old boy,' the steward greeted me. 'But he sure is sold on you!'

"Think of it! I had been drumming at that man for four years—trying to get his business—and I'd still be drumming at him if I hadn't finally taken the trouble to find out what *he* was interested in, and what *he* enjoyed talking about."

So, if you want to make people like you, **Rule 5** is:

Talk in terms of the other man's interests.

CHAPTER SIX

How to Make People Like You Instantly

I WAS WAITING in line to register a letter in the Post Office at Thirty-third Street and Eighth Avenue in New York. I noticed that the registry clerk was bored with his job—weighing envelopes, handing out the stamps, making change, issuing receipts—the same monotonous grind year after year. So I said to myself: "I am going to try to make that chap like me. Obviously, to make him like me, I must say something nice, not about myself, but about him." So I asked myself, "What is there about him that I can honestly admire?" That is sometimes a hard question to answer, especially with strangers; but, in this case, it happened to be easy. I instantly saw something I admired no end.

So while he was weighing my envelope, I remarked with enthusiasm: "I certainly wish I had your head of hair."

He looked up, half-startled, his face beaming with smiles. "Well, it isn't as good as it used to be," he said modestly. I assured him that although it might have lost some of its pristine glory, nevertheless it was still magnificent. He was immensely pleased. We carried on a pleasant conversation and the last thing he said to me was: "Many people have admired my hair."

I'll bet that chap went out to lunch that day walking on air. I'll bet he went home that night and told his wife about it. I'll bet he looked in the mirror and said: "It *is* a beautiful head of hair."

I told this story once in public; and a man asked me afterwards: "What did you want to get out of him?"

What was I trying to get out of him!!! What was I trying to get out of him!!!

If we are so contemptibly selfish that we can't radiate a little happiness and pass on a bit of honest appreciation without trying to screw something out of the other person in return—if our souls are no bigger than sour crab apples, we shall meet with the failure we so richly deserve.

Oh yes, I did want something out of that chap. I wanted something priceless. And I got it. I got the feeling that I had done something for him without his being able to do anything whatever in return for me. That is a feeling that glows and sings in your memory long after the incident has passed.

There is one all-important law of human conduct. If we obey that law, we shall almost never get into trouble. In fact, that law, if obeyed, will bring us countless friends and constant happiness. But the very instant we break that law, we shall get into endless trouble. The law is this: *Always make the other person feel important.* Professor John Dewey, as we have already noted, says that the desire to be important is the deepest urge in human nature; and Professor William James says: "The deepest principle in human nature is the craving to be appreciated." As I have already pointed out, it is the urge that differentiates us from the animals. It is the urge that has been responsible for civilization itself.

Philosophers have been speculating on the rules of human relationships for thousands of years and out of all that speculation, there has evolved only one important precept. It is not new. It is as old as history. Zoroaster taught it to his fire-worshipers in Persia three thousand years ago. Confucius preached it in China twenty-four centuries ago. Lao-tse, the founder of Taoism, taught it to his disciples in the Valley of the Han. Buddha preached it on the banks of the Holy Ganges five hundred years before Christ. The sacred books of Hinduism taught it a thousand years before that. Jesus taught it among the stony hills of Judea nineteen centuries ago. Jesus summed it up in one thought—probably the most important rule in the world: "Do unto others as you would have others do unto you."

You want the approval of those with whom you come in contact. You want recognition of your true worth. You want a feeling that you are important in your little world. You don't want to listen to cheap, insincere flattery but you do crave sincere appreciation. You want your friends and associates to be, as Charles Schwab puts it, "hearty in their appreciation and lavish in their praise." All of us want that.

So let's obey the Golden Rule, and give unto others what we would have others give unto us.

How? When? Where? The answer is: all the time, everywhere.

For example, I asked the information clerk in Radio City for the number of Henry Souvaine's office. Dressed in a neat uniform, he prided himself on the way he dispensed knowledge. Clearly and distinctly he replied: "Henry Souvaine. (pause) 18th floor. (pause) Room 1816."

I rushed for the elevator, then paused and went back and said: "I want to congratulate you on the splendid way you answered my question. You were very clear and precise. You did it like an artist. And that's unusual."

Beaming with pleasure, he told me why he made each pause, and precisely why each phrase was uttered as it was. My few words made him carry his necktie a bit higher; and as I shot up to the eighteenth floor, I got a feeling of having added a trifle to the sum total of human happiness that afternoon.

You don't have to wait until you are ambassador to France or chairman of the Clambake Committee of the Elks' Club before you use this philosophy of appreciation. You can work magic with it almost every day.

If, for example, the waitress brings us mashed potatoes when we ordered French fried, let's say: "I'm sorry to trouble you, I prefer French fried." She'll reply, "No trouble at all," and will be glad to do it because you have shown respect for her.

Little phrases such as "I'm sorry to trouble you," "Would you be so kind as to—," "Won't you please," "Would you mind," "Thank you"—little courtesies like that oil the cogs of the monotonous grind of everyday life —and, incidentally, they are the hall mark of good breeding.

Let's take another illustration. Did you ever read any of Hall Caine's novels—*The Christian, The Deemster, The Manxman?* Millions of people read his novels, countless millions. He was the son of a blacksmith. He never had more than eight years' schooling in his life, yet when he died he was the richest literary man the world has ever known.

The story goes like this: Hall Caine loved sonnets and ballads: so he devoured all of Dante Gabriel Rossetti's poetry. He even wrote a lecture chanting the praises of Rossetti's artistic achievements—and sent a copy to Rossetti himself. Rossetti was delighted. "Any young man who has such an exalted opinion of my ability," Rossetti probably said to himself, "must be brilliant." So Rossetti invited this blacksmith's son to come to London and act as his secretary. That was the turning point in Hall Caine's life; for, in his new position, he met the literary artists of the day. Profiting by their advice and inspired by their encouragement, he launched upon a career that emblazoned his name across the sky.

His home, Greeba Castle, on the Isle of Man, became a Mecca for tourists from the far corners of the world; and he left an estate of two million, five hundred thousand dollars. Yet—who knows—he might have died poor and unknown had he not written an essay expressing his admiration for a famous man.

Such is the power, the stupendous power, of sincere, heartfelt appreciation.

Rossetti considered himself important. That is not strange. Almost everyone considers himself important, very important.

So does every nation.

Do you feel that you are superior to the Japanese? The truth is that the Japanese consider themselves far superior to you. A conservative Japanese, for example, is infuriated at the sight of a white man dancing with a Japanese lady.

Do you consider yourself superior to the Hindus in India? That is your privilege; but a million Hindus feel so infinitely superior to you that they wouldn't befoul themselves by condescending to touch food that your heathen shadow had fallen across and contaminated.

Do you feel you are superior to the Eskimos? Again, that is your privilege; but would you really like to know what the Eskimo thinks of you? Well, there are a few native hobos among the Eskimos, worthless bums who refuse to work. The Eskimos call them "white men"—that being their utmost term of contempt.

Each nation feels superior to other nations. That breeds patriotism—and wars.

The unvarnished truth is that almost every man you meet feels himself superior to you in some way; and a sure way to his heart is to let him realize in some subtle way that you recognize his importance in his little world, and recognize it sincerely.

Remember what Emerson said: "Every man I meet is in some way my superior; and in that I can learn of him."

And the pathetic part of it is that frequently those who have the least justification for a feeling of achievement bolster up their inner feeling of inadequacy by an outward shouting and tumult and conceit that are offensive and truly nauseating.

As Shakespeare put it: "Man, proud man! dressed in a

little brief authority, plays such fantastic tricks before high heaven as to make the angels weep."

I am going to tell you three stories of how business men in my own courses have applied these principles with remarkable results. Let's take the case first of a Connecticut attorney who prefers not to have his name mentioned because of his relatives. We'll call him Mr. R.

Shortly after joining the course, he motored down to Long Island with his wife to visit some of her relatives. She left him to chat with an old aunt of hers and then rushed off by herself to visit some of her younger relatives. Since he had to make a talk on how he had applied the principles of appreciation, he thought he would begin with the old lady. So he looked around the house to see what he could honestly admire.

"This house was built about 1890, wasn't it?" he inquired.

"Yes," she replied, "that is precisely the year it was built."

"It reminds me of the house in which I was born," he said. "It is beautiful. Well built. Roomy. You know, they don't build houses like this any more."

"You're right," the old lady agreed. "The young folks nowadays don't care for beautiful homes. All they want is a small apartment and an electric ice box and then they go off gadding about in their automobiles.

"This is a dream house," she said in a voice vibrating with tender memories. "This house was built with love. My husband and I dreamed about it for years before we built it. We didn't have an architect. We planned it all ourselves."

She then showed him about the house, and he expressed his hearty admiration for all the beautiful treasures she had picked up in her travels and cherished over a lifetime: Paisley shawls, an old English tea set, Wedgwood china, French beds and chairs, Italian paintings, and silk draperies that had once hung in a French château.

"After showing me through the house," said Mr. R.,

"she took me out to the garage. There, jacked up on blocks, was a Packard car—almost new."

"My husband bought that car shortly before he passed on," she said softly. "I have never ridden in it since his death. . . . You appreciate nice things, and I'm going to give this car to you."

"Why, aunty," he said, "you overwhelm me. I appreciate your generosity, of course; but I couldn't possibly accept it. I'm not even a relative of yours. I have a new car; and you have many relatives that would like to have that Packard."

"Relatives!" she exclaimed. "Yes, I have relatives who are just waiting till I die so they can get that car. But they are not going to get it."

"If you don't want to give it to them, you can very easily sell it to a second-hand dealer," he told her.

"Sell it!" she cried. "Do you think I would sell this car? Do you think I could stand to see strangers riding up and down the street in that car—that car that my husband bought for me? I wouldn't dream of selling it. I am going to give it to you. You appreciate beautiful things!"

He tried to get out of accepting the car; but he couldn't without hurting her feelings.

This old lady, left in a big house all alone with her Paisley shawls, her French antiques, and her memories, was starving for a little recognition. She had once been young and beautiful and sought after. She had once built a house warm with love and had collected things from all over Europe to make it beautiful. Now, in the isolated loneliness of old age, she craved a little human warmth, a little genuine appreciation—and no one gave it to her. And when she found it, like a spring in the desert, her gratitude couldn't adequately express itself with anything less than the gift of a Packard car.

Let's take another case: Donald M. McMahon, superintendent of Lewis & Valentine, nurserymen and landscape architects in Rye, New York, related this incident:

"Shortly after I heard the talk on 'How to Win Friends and Influence People,' I was landscaping the estate of a famous attorney. The owner came out to give me a few suggestions about where he wished to plant a mass of rhododendrons and azaleas.

"I said, 'Judge, you have a lovely hobby. I have been admiring your beautiful dogs. I understand you win a lot of blue ribbons every year at the big dog show in Madison Square Garden.'

"The effect of this little expression of appreciation was striking.

" 'Yes,' the judge replied, 'I do have a lot of fun with my dogs. Wouldn't you like to see my kennel?'

"He spent almost an hour showing me his dogs and the prizes they had won. He even brought out their pedigrees and explained the blood lines responsible for such beauty and intelligence.

"Finally, turning to me, he asked: 'Do you have a little boy?'

" 'Yes, I do,' I replied.

" 'Well, wouldn't he like a puppy?' the judge inquired.

" 'Oh, yes, he'd be tickled pink.'

" 'All right, I am going to give him one,' the judge announced.

"He started to tell me how to feed the puppy. Then he paused. 'You'll forget it if I tell you. I'll write it out.' So the judge went in the house, typed out the pedigree and feeding instructions and gave me a puppy worth a hundred dollars and one hour and fifteen minutes of his valuable time largely because I expressed my honest admiration for his hobby and achievements."

George Eastman, of Kodak fame, invented the transparent film that made motion pictures possible, amassed a fortune of a hundred million dollars, and made himself one of the most famous business men on earth. Yet in spite of all these tremendous accomplishments, he craved little recognitions even as you and I.

To illustrate: A number of years ago, Eastman was building the Eastman School of Music in Rochester and also Kilbourn Hall, a theatre in memory of his mother. James Adamson, president of the Superior Seating Company of New York, wanted to get the order to supply the theatre chairs for these buildings. Phoning the architect, Mr. Adamson made an appointment to see Mr. Eastman in Rochester.

When Adamson arrived, the architect said: "I know you want to get this order; but I can tell you right now that you won't stand a ghost of a show if you take more than five minutes of George Eastman's time. He is a martinet. He is very busy. So tell your story quickly and get out."

Adamson was prepared to do just that.

When he was ushered into the room, he noticed Mr. Eastman bending over a pile of papers at his desk. Presently, Mr. Eastman looked up, removed his glasses, and walked toward the architect and Mr. Adamson, saying: "Good morning, gentlemen, what can I do for you?"

The architect introduced them and then Mr. Adamson said:

While we have been waiting for you, Mr. Eastman, I have been admiring your office. I wouldn't mind working myself if I had a room like this to work in. You know I am in the interior-woodworking business myself, and I never saw a more beautiful office in all my life.

George Eastman replied:

You remind me of something I had almost forgotten. It is beautiful, isn't it? I enjoyed it a great deal when it was first built. But I come down here now with a lot of other things on my mind and sometimes don't even see the room for weeks at a time.

Adamson walked over and rubbed his hand across a panel. "This is English oak, isn't it? A little different texture from Italian oak."

"Yes," Eastman replied. "That is imported English oak. It was selected for me by a friend who specializes in fine woods."

Then Eastman showed him about the room, pointing out the proportions, the coloring, the hand carving and other effects that he had helped to plan and execute.

While drifting about the room, admiring the woodwork, they paused before a window and George Eastman, in his modest, soft-spoken way, pointed out some of the institutions through which he was trying to help humanity: the University of Rochester, the General Hospital, the Homeopathic Hospital, the Friendly Home, the Children's Hospital. Mr. Adamson congratulated him warmly on the idealistic way he was using his wealth to alleviate the sufferings of humanity. Presently George Eastman unlocked a glass case and pulled out the first camera he had ever owned—an invention he had bought from an Englishman.

Adamson questioned him at length about his early struggles to get started in business, and Mr. Eastman spoke with real feeling about the poverty of his childhood, told how his widowed mother had kept a boarding house while he clerked in an insurance office for fifty cents a day. The terror of poverty haunted him day and night and he resolved to make enough money so his mother wouldn't have to work herself to death in a boarding house. Mr. Adamson drew him out with further questions and listened, absorbed, while he related the story of his experiments with dry photographic plates. He told how he had worked in an office all day, and sometimes experimented all night, taking only brief naps while the chemicals were working, sometimes working and sleeping in his clothes for seventy-two hours at a stretch.

James Adamson had been ushered into Eastman's office at 10:15, and warned that he must not take more than five minutes; but an hour passed, two hours passed. They were still talking.

Finally, George Eastman turned to Adamson and said, "The last time I was in Japan I bought some chairs, brought them home, and put them in my sun porch. But the sun peeled the paint, so I went down town the other day and bought some paint and painted the chairs myself. Would you like to see what sort of a job I can do painting chairs? All right. Come up to my home and have lunch with me and I'll show you."

After lunch, Mr. Eastman showed Adamson the chairs

he had brought from Japan. They weren't worth more than $1.50 apiece, but George Eastman, who had made a hundred million dollars in business, was proud of them because he himself had painted them.

The order for the seats amounted to $90,000. Who do you suppose got the order—James Adamson or one of his competitors?

From that time on until Mr. Eastman's death, he and James Adamson were close friends.

Where should you and I begin applying this magic touchstone of appreciation? Why not begin right at home? I don't know of any other place where it is more needed —or more neglected. Your wife must have some good points—at least you once thought she had or you wouldn't have married her. But how long has it been since you expressed your admiration for her attractions? How long?? How long????

I was fishing up on the headwaters of the Miramichi in New Brunswick a few years ago. I was isolated in a lonely camp deep in the Canadian woods. The only thing I could find to read was a country newspaper. I read everything in it, including the ads and an article by Dorothy Dix. Her article was so fine that I cut it out and kept it. She claimed she was tired of always hearing lectures to brides. She declared that someone ought to take the bridegroom to one side and give him this bit of sage advice:

Never get married until you have kissed the Blarney Stone. Praising a woman before marriage is a matter of inclination. But praising one after you marry her is a matter of necessity—and personal safety. Matrimony is no place for candor. It is a field for diplomacy.

If you wish to fare sumptuously every day, never knock your wife's housekeeping or make invidious comparisons between it and your mother's. But, on the contrary, be forever praising her domesticity and openly congratulate yourself upon having married the only woman who combines the attractions of Venus and Minerva and Mary Ann. Even when the steak is leather and the bread a cinder, don't complain. Merely remark that the meal isn't up to her usual standard of perfection, and she will make a burnt offering of herself on the kitchen stove to live up to your ideal of her.

Don't begin this too suddenly—or she'll be suspicious. But tonight, or tomorrow night bring her some flowers or a box of candy. Don't merely say, "Yes, I ought to do it." *Do it!* And bring her a smile in addition, and some warm words of affection. If more wives and more husbands did that, I wonder if we should still have one marriage out of every six shattered on the rocks of Reno?

Would you like to know how to make a woman fall in love with you? Well, here is the secret. This is going to be good. It is not my idea. I borrowed it from Dorothy Dix. She once interviewed a celebrated bigamist who had won the hearts and savings-bank accounts of twenty-three women. (And, by the way, it ought to be noted in passing that she interviewed him in jail.) When she asked him his recipe for making women fall in love with him, he said it was no trick at all; all you had to do was to talk to a woman about herself.

And the same technique works with men: "Talk to a man about himself," said Disraeli, one of the shrewdest men who ever ruled the British Empire, "talk to a man about himself and he will listen for hours."

So if you want people to like you, **Rule 6** is:

Make the other person feel important—and do it sincerely.

You've been reading this book long enough. Close it now, knock the dead ashes out of your pipe, and begin to apply this philosophy of appreciation at once on the person nearest you—and watch the magic work.

IN A NUTSHELL

Six Ways to Make People Like You

RULE 1: Become genuinely interested in other people.

RULE 2: Smile.

RULE 3: Remember that a man's name is to him the sweetest and most important sound in any language.

RULE 4: Be a good listener. Encourage others to talk about themselves.

RULE 5: Talk in terms of the other man's interest.

RULE 6: Make the other person feel important —and do it sincerely.

PART THREE

Twelve Ways to Win People to Your Way of Thinking

CHAPTER ONE

You Can't Win an Argument

SHORTLY AFTER the close of the war, I learned an invaluable lesson one night in London. I was manager at the time for Sir Ross Smith. During the war, Sir Ross had been the Australian ace out in Palestine; and, shortly after peace was declared, he astonished the world by flying halfway around it in thirty days. No such feat had ever been attempted before. It created a tremendous sensation. The Australian government gave him fifty thousand dollars; the King of England knighted him; and, for awhile, he was the most talked-of man under the Union Jack—the Lindbergh of the British Empire. I was attending a banquet one night given in Sir Ross's honor; and during the dinner, the man sitting next to me told a humorous story which hinged on the quotation, "There's a divinity that shapes our ends, rough-hew them how we will."

The raconteur mentioned that the quotation was from the Bible. He was wrong. I knew that. I knew it positively. There couldn't be the slightest doubt about it. And so, to get a feeling of importance and display my superiority, I appointed myself an unsolicited and unwelcome committee

111

of one to correct him. He stuck to his guns. What? From Shakespeare? Impossible! Absurd! That quotation was from the Bible. And he knew it!

The story-teller was sitting on my right; and Mr. Frank Gammond, an old friend of mine, was seated at my left. Mr. Gammond had devoted years to the study of Shakespeare. So the story-teller and I agreed to submit the question to Mr. Gammond. Mr. Gammond listened, kicked me under the table, and then said: "Dale, you are wrong. The gentleman is right. It *is* from the Bible."

On our way home that night, I said to Mr. Gammond: "Frank, you knew that quotation was from Shakespeare."

"Yes, of course," he replied, "Hamlet, Act V, Scene 2. But we were guests at a festive occasion, my dear Dale. Why prove to a man he is wrong? Is that going to make him like you? Why not let him save his face? He didn't ask for your opinion. He didn't want it. Why argue with him? Always avoid the acute angle."

"Always avoid the acute angle." The man who said that is now dead; but the lesson that he taught me goes marching on.

It was a sorely needed lesson because I had been an inveterate arguer. During my youth, I had argued with my brother about everything under the Milky Way. When I went to college, I studied logic and argumentation, and went in for debating contests. Talk about being from Missouri, I was born there. I had to be shown. Later, I taught debating and argumentation in New York; and once, I am ashamed to admit, I planned to write a book on the subject. Since then, I have listened to, criticized, engaged in, and watched the effects of thousands of arguments. As a result of it all, I have come to the conclusion that there is only one way under high heaven to get the best of an argument—and that is to avoid it. Avoid it as you would avoid rattlesnakes and earthquakes.

Nine times out of ten, an argument ends with each of the contestants being more firmly convinced than ever that he is absolutely right.

You can't win an argument. You can't because if you lose it, you lose it; and if you win it, you lose it. Why?

Well, suppose you triumph over the other man and shoot his argument full of holes and prove that he is *non compos mentis*. Then what? You will feel fine. But what about him? You have made him feel inferior. You have hurt his pride. He will resent your triumph. And—

> *"A man convinced against his will*
> *Is of the same opinion still."*

The Penn Mutual Life Insurance Company has laid down a definite policy for its salesmen: "Don't argue!"

Real salesmanship isn't argument. It isn't anything even remotely like argument. The human mind isn't changed that way.

To illustrate: Years ago, a belligerent Irishman by the name of Patrick J. O'Haire joined one of my classes. He had had little education, and how he loved a scrap! He had once been a chauffeur, and he came to me because he had been trying, without much success, to sell automobile trucks. A little questioning brought out the fact that he was continually scrapping with and antagonizing the very people he was trying to do business with. If a prospect said anything derogatory about the trucks he was selling, Pat saw red and was right at the man's throat. Pat won a lot of arguments in those days. As he said to me afterwards, "I often walked out of a man's office saying: 'I told that bird something.' Sure I had told him something, but I hadn't sold him anything."

My first problem was not to teach Patrick J. O'Haire to talk. My immediate task was to train him to refrain from talking and to avoid verbal fights.

Mr. O'Haire is now one of the star salesmen for the White Motor Company in New York. How does he do it? Here is his story in his own words: "If I walk into a buyer's office now and he says: 'What? A White truck? They're no good! I wouldn't take one if you gave it to me. I'm going to buy the Whoseit truck,' I say, 'Brother, listen, the Whoseit is a good truck. If you buy the Whoseit you'll never make a mistake. The Whoseits are made by a fine company and sold by good people.'

"He is speechless then. There is no room for an argument. If he says the Whoseit is best and I say sure it is, he has to stop. He can't keep on all afternoon saying, 'It's the best' when I'm agreeing with him. We then get off the subject of Whoseit and I begin to talk about the good points of the White truck.

"There was a time when a crack like that would make me see scarlet and red and orange. I would start arguing against the Whoseit; and the more I argued against it, the more my prospect argued in favor of it; and the more he argued, the more he sold himself on my competitor's product.

"As I look back now I wonder how I was ever able to sell anything. I lost years of my life in scrapping and arguing. I keep my mouth shut now. It pays."

As wise old Ben Franklin used to say:

> If you argue and rankle and contradict, you may achieve a victory sometimes; but it will be an empty victory because you will never get your opponent's good will.

So figure it out for yourself. Which would you rather have: an academic, theatrical victory or a man's good will? You can seldom have both.

The Boston Transcript once printed this bit of significant doggerel:

> *"Here lies the body of William Jay,*
> *Who died maintaining his right of way—*
> *He was right, dead right, as he sped along,*
> *But he's just as dead as if he were wrong."*

You may be right, dead right, as you speed along in your argument; but as far as changing the other man's mind is concerned, you will probably be just as futile as if you were wrong.

William G. McAdoo, Secretary of the Treasury in Woodrow Wilson's cabinet, declared that he had learned, as a result of his crowded years in politics, that "it is impossible to defeat an ignorant man by argument."

"An ignorant man?" You put it mildly, Mr. McAdoo. My experience has been that it is all but impossible to make *any* man—regardless of his I. Q. rating—change his mind by a verbal joust.

For example, Frederick S. Parsons, an income-tax consultant, had been disputing and wrangling for an hour with a government tax inspector. An item of nine thousand dollars was at stake. Mr. Parsons claimed that this nine thousand was in reality a bad debt, that it would never be collected, that it ought not to be taxed. "Bad debt, my eye!" retorted the inspector. "It must be taxed."

"This inspector was cold, arrogant, and stubborn," Mr. Parsons said as he told the story to the class. "Reason was wasted on him and so were facts. . . . The longer we argued, the more stubborn he became. So I decided to avoid argument, change the subject, and give him appreciation.

"I said, 'I suppose that this is a very petty matter in comparison with the really important and difficult decisions you are required to make. I've made a study of taxation myself. But I've had to get my knowledge from books. You are getting yours from the firing line of experience. I sometimes wish I had a job like yours. It would teach me a lot.' I meant every word I said.

"Well, the inspector straightened up in his chair, leaned back, and talked for a long time about his work, telling me of the clever frauds he had uncovered. His tone gradually became friendly; and presently he was telling me about his children. As he left, he advised me that he would consider my problem further, and give me his decision in a few days.

"He called at my office three days later and informed me that he had decided to leave the tax return exactly as it was filed."

This tax inspector was demonstrating one of the most common of human frailties. He wanted a feeling of importance; and as long as Mr. Parsons argued with him, he got his feeling of importance by loudly asserting his authority. But as soon as his importance was admitted, and the argument stopped, and he was permitted to expand his ego, he became a sympathetic and kindly human being.

Constant, the head valet in Napoleon's household, often played billiards with Josephine. Constant says on page 73, Volume I, of his *Recollections of the Private Life of Napoleon:* "Although I had some skill, I always managed to let her beat me, which pleased her exceedingly."

Let's learn a constant lesson from Constant. Let's let our customers and sweethearts and husbands and wives beat us in the little discussions that may arise.

Buddha said: "Hatred is never ended by hatred but by love," and a misunderstanding is never ended by an argument but by tact, diplomacy, conciliation, and a sympathetic desire to see the other person's viewpoint.

Lincoln once reprimanded a young army officer for indulging in a violent controversy with an associate. "No man who is resolved to make the most of himself," said Lincoln, "can spare time for personal contention. Still less can he afford to take the consequences, including the vitiation of his temper and the loss of self-control. Yield larger things to which you show no more than equal rights; and yield lesser ones though clearly your own. Better give your path to a dog than be bitten by him in contesting for the right. Even killing the dog would not cure the bite."

Therefore, **Rule 1** is:

The only way to get the best of an argument is to avoid it.

CHAPTER TWO

A Sure Way of Making Enemies— and How to Avoid It

WHEN Theodore Roosevelt was in the White House, he confessed that if he could be right 75 per cent of the time, he would reach the highest measure of his expectations.

If that was the highest rating that one of the most distinguished men of the twentieth century could hope to obtain, what about you and me?

If you can be sure of being right only 55 per cent of the time, you can go down to Wall Street, make a million dollars a day, buy a yacht, and marry a chorus girl. And if you can't be sure of being right even 55 per cent of the time, why should you tell other people they are wrong?

You can tell a man he is wrong by a look or an intonation or a gesture just as eloquently as you can in words— and if you tell him he is wrong, do you make him want to agree with you? Never! For you have struck a direct blow at his intelligence, his judgment, his pride, his self-respect. That will make him want to strike back. But it will never make him want to change his mind. You may then hurl

117

at him all the logic of a Plato or an Immanuel Kant, but you will not alter his opinion, for you have hurt his feelings.

Never begin by announcing, "I am going to prove so and so to you." That's bad. That's tantamount to saying: "I'm smarter than you are. I'm going to tell you a thing or two and make you change your mind."

That is a challenge. That arouses opposition, and makes the listener want to battle with you before you even start.

It is difficult, under even the most benign conditions, to change people's minds. So why make it harder? Why handicap yourself?

If you are going to prove anything, don't let anybody know it. Do it so subtly, so adroitly that no one will feel that you are doing it.

> "Men must be taught as if you taught them not
> And things unknown proposed as things forgot."

As Lord Chesterfield said to his son:

> Be wiser than other people, if you can; but do not tell them so.

I believe now hardly anything that I believed twenty years ago—except the multiplication table; and I begin to doubt even that when I read about Einstein. In another twenty years, I may not believe what I have said in this book. I am not so sure now of anything as I used to be. Socrates said repeatedly to his followers in Athens: "One thing only I know; and that is that I know nothing."

Well, I can't hope to be any smarter than Socrates; so I have quit telling people they are wrong. And I find that it pays.

If a man makes a statement that you think is wrong— yes, even that you know is wrong—isn't it better to begin by saying: "Well, now, look! I thought otherwise, but I may be wrong. I frequently am. And if I am wrong, I want to be put right. Let's examine the facts"?

There's magic, positive magic, in such phrases as: "I may be wrong. I frequently am. Let's examine the facts."

Nobody in the heavens above or the earth beneath or in the waters under the earth will ever object to your saying: "I may be wrong. Let's examine the facts."

That is what a scientist does. I once interviewed Stefansson, the famous explorer and scientist who spent eleven years up beyond the Arctic Circle and who lived on absolutely nothing but meat and water for six years. He told me of a certain experiment he had conducted and I asked him what he tried to prove by it. I shall never forget his reply. He said: "A scientist never tries to prove anything. He attempts only to find the facts."

You like to be scientific in your thinking, don't you? Well, no one is stopping you but yourself.

You will never get into trouble by admitting that you may be wrong. That will stop all argument and inspire the other fellow to be just as fair and open and broadminded as you are. It will make him want to admit that he, too, may be wrong.

If you know positively that a man is wrong, and you tell him so bluntly, what happens? Let me illustrate by a specific case. Mr. S——, a young New York attorney, was arguing a rather important case recently before the United States Supreme Court (*Lustgarten v. Fleet Corporation,* 280 U.S. 320). The case involved a considerable sum of money and an important question of law.

During the argument, one of the Supreme Court justices said to Mr. S——: "The statue of limitations in admiralty law is six years, is it not?"

Mr. S—— stopped, stared at Justice —— for a moment, and then said bluntly: "Your Honor, there is no statute of limitations in admiralty."

"A hush fell on the court," said Mr. S——, as he related his experience to one of the author's classes, "and the temperature in the room seemed to go down to zero. I was right. Justice —— was wrong. And I had told him so. But did that make him friendly? No. I still believe that

I had the law on my side. And I know that I spoke better than I ever spoke before. But I didn't persuade. I made the enormous blunder of telling a very learned and famous man that he was wrong."

Few people are logical. Most of us are prejudiced and biased. Most of us are blighted with preconceived notions, with jealousy, suspicion, fear, envy, and pride. And most citizens don't want to change their minds about their religion or their hair cut or Communism or Clark Gable. So, if you are inclined to tell people they are wrong, please read the following paragraph on your knees every morning before breakfast. It is from Professor James Harvey Robinson's enlightening book, *The Mind in the Making*.

We sometimes find ourselves changing our minds without any resistance or heavy emotion, but if we are told we are wrong, we resent the imputation and harden our hearts. We are incredibly heedless in the formation of our beliefs, but find ourselves filled with an illicit passion for them when anyone proposes to rob us of their companionship. It is obviously not the ideas themselves that are dear to us, but our self-esteem which is threatened. . . . The little word "my" is the most important one in human affairs, and properly to reckon with it is the beginning of wisdom. It has the same force whether it is "my" dinner, "my" dog, and "my" house, or "my" father, "my" country, and "my" God. We not only resent the imputation that our watch is wrong, or our car shabby, but that our conception of the canals of Mars, of the pronunciation of "Epictetus," of the medicinal value of salicin, or of the date of Sargon I is subject to revision . . . We like to continue to believe what we have been accustomed to accept as true, and the resentment aroused when doubt is cast upon any of our assumptions leads us to seek every manner of excuse for clinging to it. The result is that most of our so-called reasoning consists in finding arguments for going on believing as we already do.

I once employed an interior decorator to make some draperies for my home. When the bill arrived, I caught my breath.

A few days later, a friend called and looked at the drapes. The price was mentioned and she exclaimed with a note of triumph: "What? That's awful. I am afraid he put one over on you."

True? Yes, she had told the truth, but few people like to listen to truths that reflect on their judgment. So, being human, I tried to defend myself. I pointed out that the best is eventually the cheapest, that one can't expect to get quality and artistic taste at bargain-basement prices, and so on and on.

The next day another friend dropped in, admired the draperies, bubbled over with enthusiasm, and expressed a wish that she could afford such exquisite creations for her home. My reaction was totally different. "Well, to tell the truth," I said, "I can't afford them myself. I paid too much. I'm sorry I ordered them."

When we are wrong, we may admit it to ourselves. And if we are handled gently and tactfully, we may admit it to others and even take pride in our frankness and broadmindedness. But not if someone else is trying to ram the unpalatable fact down our esophagus. . . .

Horace Greeley, the most famous editor in America during the time of the Civil War, disagreed violently with Lincoln's policies. He believed that he could drive Lincoln into agreeing with him by a campaign of argument, ridicule, and abuse. He waged this bitter campaign month after month, year after year. In fact, he wrote a brutal, bitter, sarcastic and personal attack on President Lincoln the night Booth shot him.

But did all this bitterness make Lincoln agree with Greeley? Not at all. Ridicule and abuse never do.

If you want some excellent suggestions about dealing with people and managing yourself and improving your personality, read Benjamin Franklin's autobiography—one of the most fascinating life stories ever written, one of the classics of American literature. Borrow a copy from your public library or get a copy from your bookstore.

If there is no bookstore in your town, you can order one direct from Pocket Books Mail Service Department, 1 West 39th Street, New York City. Ask for the *Autobiography of Benjamin Franklin*. The price is $1.25 and enclose 35c for postage and handling.

In this autobiography, Ben Franklin tells how he conquered the iniquitous habit of argument and transformed himself into one of the most able, suave, and diplomatic men in American history.

One day, when Ben Franklin was a blundering youth, an old Quaker friend took him aside and lashed him with a few stinging truths, something like this:

> Ben, you are impossible. Your opinions have a slap in them for everyone who differs with you. They have become so expensive that nobody cares for them. Your friends find they enjoy themselves better when you are not around. You know so much that no man can tell you anything. Indeed, no man is going to try, for the effort would lead only to discomfort and hard work. So you are not likely ever to know any more than you do now, which is very little.

One of the finest things I know about Ben Franklin is the way that he accepted that smarting rebuke. He was big enough and wise enough to realize it was true, to sense that he was headed for failure and social disaster. So he made a right-about-face. He began immediately to change his insolent, bigoted ways.

"I made it a rule," said Franklin, "to forbear all direct contradiction to the sentiments of others, and all positive assertion of my own. I even forbade myself the use of every word or expression in the language that imported a fix'd opinion, such as 'certainly,' 'undoubtedly,' etc., and I adopted, instead of them, 'I conceive,' 'I apprehend,' or 'I imagine' a thing to be so or so; or 'it so appears to me at present.' When another asserted something that I thought an error, I deny'd myself the pleasure of contradicting him abruptly, and of showing immediately some absurdity in his proposition: and in answering I began by observing that in certain cases or circumstances his opinion would be right, but in the present case there appear'd or seem'd to me some difference, etc. I soon found the advantage of this change in my manner; the conversations I engag'd in went on more pleasantly. The modest way in which I propos'd my opinions procur'd them a readier reception and less contradiction; I had less mortification when I was found to be in the wrong, and I more easily prevail'd with others to give up their mistakes and join with me when I happened to be in the right.

"And this mode, which I at first put on with some violence to natural inclination, became at length so easy, and so habitual to me, that perhaps for these fifty years past no one has ever heard a dogmatical expression escape me. And to this habit (after my character of integrity) I think it principally owing that I had early so much weight with my fellow citizens when I proposed new institutions, or alterations in the old, and so much influence in public councils when I became a member; for I was but a bad speaker, never eloquent, subject to much hesitation in my choice of words, hardly correct in language, and yet I generally carried my points."

How do Ben Franklin's methods work in business? Let's take two examples.

F. J. Mahoney, of 114 Liberty Street, New York, sells special equipment for the oil trade. He had booked an order for an important customer in Long Island. A blue print had been submitted and approved, and the equipment was in the process of fabrication. Then an unfortunate thing happened. The buyer discussed the matter with his friends. They warned him he was making a grave mistake. He had had something pawned off on him that was all wrong. It was too wide, too short, too this and too that. His friends worried him into a temper. Calling Mr. Mahoney on the phone, he swore he wouldn't accept the equipment that was already being manufactured.

"I checked things over very carefully and knew positively that we were right," said Mr. Mahoney as he told the story, "and I also knew that he and his friends didn't know what they were talking about, but I sensed that it would be dangerous to tell him so. I went out to Long Island to see him, and as I walked into his office, he leaped to his feet and came oward me, talking rapidly. He was so excited that he shook his fist as he talked. He condemned me and my equipment and ended up by saying, 'Now, what are you going to do about it?'

"I told him very calmly that I would do anything he said. 'You are the man who is going to pay for this,' I said, 'so you should certainly get what you want. However, somebody has to accept the responsibility. If you think you are right, give us a blue print and, although we have spent $2,000 making this job for you, we'll scrap that. We are willing to lose $2,000 in order to please you. However, I must warn you that if we build it as you insist, you must take the responsibility. But if you let us proceed as we planned, which we still believe is the right way, we will assume the responsibility.'

"He had calmed down by this time, and finally said: 'All right, go ahead, but if it is not right, God help you.'

"It was right, and he has already promised us another order for two similar jobs this season.

"When this man insulted me and shook his fist in my face and told me I didn't know my business, it took all the self-control I could summon up not to argue and try to justify myself. It took a lot of self-control, but it paid. If I had told him he was wrong and started an argument, there probably would have been a law suit, bitter feelings, a financial loss, and the loss of a valuable customer. Yes, I am convinced that it doesn't pay to tell a man he is wrong."

Let's take another example—and remember these cases I am citing are typical of the experiences of thousands of other men. R. V. Crowley is a salesman for the Gardner W. Taylor Lumber Company, of New York. Crowley admitted that he had been telling hard-boiled lumber inspectors for years that they were wrong. And he had won the arguments too. But it hadn't done any good. "For these lumber inspectors," said Mr. Crowley, "are like baseball umpires. Once they make a decision, they never change it."

Mr. Crowley saw that his firm was losing thousands of dollars through the arguments he won. So while taking my course, he resolved to change tactics and abandon arguments. With what results? Here is the story as he told it to the fellow members of his class:

One morning the phone rang in my office. A hot and bothered person at the other end proceeded to inform me that a car of lumber we had shipped into his plant was entirely unsatisfactory. His firm had stopped unloading and requested that we make immediate arrangements to remove the stock from their yard. After about one-fourth of the car had been unloaded, their lumber inspector reported that the lumber was running 55 per cent below grade. Under the circumstances, they refused to accept it.

I immediately started for his plant and on the way turned over in my mind the best way to handle the situation. Ordinarily, under such circumstances, I should have quoted grading rules and tried, as a result of my own experience and knowledge as a lumber inspector, to convince the other inspector that the lumber was actually up to grade, and that he was misinterpreting the rules in his inspection. However, I thought I would apply the principles learned in this training.

When I arrived at the plant, I found the purchasing agent and the lumber inspector in a wicked humor, all set for an argument and a fight. We walked out to the car that was being unloaded and I requested that they continue to unload so that I could see how things were going. I asked the inspector to go right ahead and lay out the rejects, as he had been doing, and to put the good pieces in another pile.

After watching him for a while it began to dawn on me that his inspection actually was much too strict and that he was misinterpreting the rules. This particular lumber was white pine, and I knew the inspector was thoroughly schooled in hard woods but not a competent, experienced inspector on white pine. White pine happened to be my own strong suit, but did I offer any objection to the way he was grading the lumber? None whatever. I kept on watching and gradually began to ask questions as to why certain pieces were not satisfactory. I didn't for one instant insinuate that the inspector was wrong. I emphasized that my only reason for asking was in order that we could give his firm exactly what they wanted in future shipments.

By asking questions in a very friendly, co-operative spirit, and insisting continually that they were right in laying out boards not satisfactory to their purpose, I got him warmed up and the strained relations between us began to thaw and melt away. An occasional carefully put remark on my part gave birth to the idea in his mind that possibly some of these rejected pieces were actually within the grade that they had bought, and that their requirements demanded a more expensive grade. I was very careful, however, not to let him think I was making an issue of this point.

Gradually his whole attitude changed. He finally admitted to me that he was not experienced on white pine and began to ask me questions about each piece as it came out of the car. I would explain why such a piece came within the grade specified, but kept on insisting that we did not want him to take it if it was unsuitable for their purpose. He finally got to the point where he felt guilty every time he put a piece in the rejected pile. And at last he saw that the mistake was on their part for not having specified as good a grade as they needed.

The ultimate outcome was that he went through the entire carload again after I left, accepted the whole lot, and we received a check in full.

In that one instance alone, a little tact and the determination to refrain from telling the other man he was wrong, saved my company one hundred and fifty dollars in actual cash, and it would be hard to place a money value on the good will that was saved.

By the way, I am not revealing anything new in this chapter. Nineteen centuries ago, Jesus said: "Agree with thine adversary quickly."

In other words, don't argue with your customer or your husband or your adversary. Don't tell him he is wrong, don't get him stirred up, but use a little diplomacy.

And 2,200 years before Christ was born, old King Akhtoi of Egypt gave his son some shrewd advice—advice that is sorely needed today. Old King Akhtoi said one afternoon, between drinks, four thousand years ago: "Be diplomatic. It will help you gain your point."

So, if you want to win people to your way of thinking, Rule 2 is:

Show respect for the other man's opinions. Never tell a man he is wrong.

CHAPTER THREE

If You're Wrong, Admit It

I LIVE almost in the geographical center of Greater New York; yet within a minute's walk of my house there is a wild stretch of virgin timber, where the blackberry thickets foam white in the springtime, where the squirrels nest and rear their young and the horseweeds grow as tall as a horse's head. This unspoiled woodland is called Forest Park—and it *is* a forest, probably not much different in appearance from what it was the afternoon Columbus discovered America. I frequently go walking in this park with Rex, my little Boston bulldog. He is a friendly, harmless little hound; and since we rarely meet anyone in the park, I take Rex along without a leash or a muzzle.

One day we encountered a mounted policeman in the park, a policeman itching to show his authority.

"What do you mean by letting that dog run loose in the park without a muzzle and leash?" he reprimanded me. "Don't you know it is against the law?"

"Yes, I know it is," I replied softly, "but I didn't think he would do any harm out here."

"You didn't *think!* You didn't *think!* The law doesn't

give a tinker's dam about what you *think*. That dog might kill a squirrel or bite a child. Now, I'm going to let you off this time; but if I catch this dog out here again without a muzzle and a leash, you'll have to tell it to the judge."

I meekly promised to obey.

And I did obey—for a few times. But Rex didn't like the muzzle, and neither did I; so we decided to take a chance. Everything was lovely for awhile; and then we struck a snag. Rex and I raced over the brow of a hill one afternoon and there, suddenly—to my dismay—I saw the majesty of the law, astride a bay horse. Rex was out in front, heading straight for the officer.

I was in for it. I knew it. So I didn't wait until the policeman started talking. I beat him to it. I said: "Officer, you've caught me red-handed. I'm guilty. I have no alibis, no excuses. You warned me last week that if I brought this dog out here again without a muzzle you would fine me."

"Well, now," the policeman responded in a soft tone. "I know it's a temptation to let a little dog like that have a run out here when nobody is around."

"Sure it's a temptation," I replied, "but it is against the law."

"Well, a little dog like that isn't going to harm anybody," the policeman remonstrated.

"No, but he may kill squirrels," I said.

"Well, now, I think you are taking this a bit too seriously," he told me. "I'll tell you what you do. You just let him run over the hill there where I can't see him—and we'll forget all about it."

That policeman, being human, wanted a feeling of importance; so when I began to condemn myself, the only way he could nourish his self-esteem was to take the magnanimous attitude of showing mercy.

But suppose I had tried to defend myself—well, did you ever argue with a policeman?

But instead of breaking lances with him, I admitted that he was absolutely right and I was absolutely wrong; I admitted it quickly, openly, and with enthusiasm. The affair terminated graciously by my taking his side and his taking my side. Lord Chesterfield himself could hardly have been more gracious than this mounted policeman who, only a week previously, had threatened to have the law on me.

If we know we are going to get the Old Harry anyhow, isn't it far better to beat the other fellow to it and do it ourselves? Isn't it much easier to listen to self-criticism than to bear condemnation from alien lips?

Say about yourself all the derogatory things you know the other person is thinking or wants to say or intends to say—and say them before he has a chance to say them—and you take the wind out of his sails. The chances are a hundred to one that he will then take a generous, forgiving attitude and minimize your mistakes—just as the mounted policeman did with me and Rex.

Ferdinand E. Warren, a commercial artist, used this technique to win the good will of a petulant, scolding buyer of art.

"It is important, in making drawings for advertising and publishing purposes, to be precise and very exact," Mr. Warren said as he told the story.

"Some art editors demand that their commissions be executed immediately; and in these cases, some slight error is liable to occur. I knew one art director in particular who was always delighted to find fault with some little thing. I have often left his office in disgust, not because of the criticism, but because of his method of attack. Recently I delivered a rush job to this editor and he phoned me to call at his office immediately. He said something was wrong. When I arrived, I found just what I had anticipated —and dreaded. He was hostile, gloating over his chance to criticize. He demanded with heat why I had done so and so. My opportunity had come to apply the self-criticism I had been studying about. So I said: 'Mr. So-and-so, if what you say is true, I am at fault and there is absolutely no excuse for my blunder. I have been doing drawings for you long enough to know better. I'm ashamed of myself.'

"Immediately he started to defend me. 'Yes, you're right, but after all, this isn't a serious mistake. It is only—'

"I interrupted him. 'Any mistake,' I said, 'may be costly and they are all irritating.'

"He started to break in; but I wouldn't let him. I was having a grand time. For the first time in my life, I was criticizing myself—and I loved it.

" 'I should have been more careful,' I continued. 'You give me a lot of work; and you deserve the best; so I'm going to do this drawing all over.'

" 'No! No!' he protested. 'I wouldn't think of putting you to all that trouble.' He praised my work, assured me that he wanted only a minor change, and that my slight error hadn't cost his firm any money; and, after all, it was a mere detail—not worth worrying about.

"My eagerness to criticize myself took all the fight out of him. He ended up by taking me to lunch; and before we parted, he gave me a check and another commission."

Any fool can try to defend his mistakes—and most fools do—but it raises one above the herd and gives one a feeling of nobility and exultation to admit one's mistakes. For example, one of the most beautiful things that history records about Robert E. Lee is the way he blamed himself and only himself for the failure of Pickett's charge at Gettysburg.

Pickett's charge was undoubtedly the most brilliant and picturesque attack that ever occurred in the western world. Pickett himself was picturesque. He wore his hair so long that his auburn locks almost touched his shoulders; and, like Napoleon in his Italian campaigns, he wrote ardent love-letters almost daily on the battlefield. His devoted troops cheered him that tragic July afternoon as he rode off jauntily toward the Union lines, with his cap set at a rakish angle over his right ear. They cheered and they followed him, man touching man, rank pressing rank, with banners flying and bayonets gleaming in the sun. It was a gallant sight. Daring. Magnificent. A murmur of admiration ran through the Union lines as they beheld it.

Pickett's troops swept forward at an easy trot, through orchard and corn-field, across a meadow, and over a ravine. All the time, the enemy's cannons were tearing ghastly holes in their ranks. But on they pressed, grim, irresistible.

Suddenly the Union infantry rose from behind the stone wall on Cemetery Ridge where they had been hiding, and fired volley after volley into Pickett's defenseless troops. The crest of the hill was a sheet of flame, a slaughter-house a blazing volcano. In a few minutes, all of Pickett's brigade commanders except one were down, and four-fifths of his five thousand men had fallen.

Armistead, leading the troops in the final plunge, ran forward, vaulted over the stone wall, and, waving his cap on the top of his sword, shouted:

"Give 'em the steel, boys!"

They did. They leaped over the wall, bayoneted their enemies, smashed skulls with clubbed muskets, and planted the battle-flags of the South on Cemetery Ridge.

The banners waved there only for a moment. But that moment, brief as it was, recorded the high-water mark of the Confederacy.

Pickett's charge—brilliant, heroic—was nevertheless the beginning of the end. Lee had failed. He could not penetrate the North and he knew it.

The South was doomed.

Lee was so saddened, so shocked, that he sent in his resignation and asked Jefferson Davis, the President of the Confederacy, to appoint "a younger and abler man." If Lee had wanted to blame the disastrous failure of Pickett's charge on someone else, he could have found a score of alibis. Some of his division commanders had failed him. The cavalry hadn't arrived in time to support the infantry attack. This had gone wrong and that had gone awry.

But Lee was far too noble to blame others. As Pickett's beaten and bloody troops struggled back to the Confederate lines, Robert E. Lee rode out to meet them all alone and greeted them with a self-condemnation that was little short of sublime. "All this has been my fault," he confessed. "I and I alone have lost this battle."

Few generals in all history have had the courage and character to admit that.

Elbert Hubbard was one of the most original authors who ever stirred up a nation, and his stinging sentences often aroused fierce resentments. But Hubbard with his rare skill for handling people frequently turned his enemies into friends.

For example, when some irritated reader wrote in to say that he didn't agree with such and such article and ended by calling Hubbard this and that, Elbert Hubbard would answer like this:

> Come to think it over, I don't entirely agree with it myself. Not everything I wrote yesterday appeals to me today. I am glad to learn what you think on the subject. The next time you are in the neighborhood you must visit us and we'll get this subject threshed out for all time. So here is a handclasp over the miles, and I am
>
> > Yours sincerely,

What could you say to a man who treated you like that?

When we are right, let's try to win people gently and tactfully to our way of thinking; and when we are wrong—and that will be surprisingly often, if we are honest with ourselves—let's admit our mistakes quickly and with enthusiasm. That technique will not only produce astonishing results; but, believe it or not, it is a lot more fun, under the circumstances, than trying to defend one's self.

Remember the old proverb: "By fighting you never get enough, but by yielding you get more than you expected."

So if you want to win people to your way of thinking, it would be advisable to remember **Rule 3**:

If you are wrong, admit it quickly and emphatically.

CHAPTER FOUR

The High Road to a Man's Reason

IF YOUR TEMPER is aroused and you tell 'em a thing or two, you will have a fine time unloading your feelings. But what about the other fellow? Will he share your pleasure? Will your belligerent tones, your hostile attitude, make it easy for him to agree with you?

"If you come at me with your fists doubled," said Woodrow Wilson, "I think I can promise you that mine will double as fast as yours; but if you come to me and say, 'Let us sit down and take counsel together, and, if we differ from one another, understand why it is that we differ from one another, just what the points at issue are,' we will presently find that we are not so far apart after all, that the points on which we differ are few and the points on which we agree are many, and that if we only have the patience and the candor and the desire to get together, we will get together."

Nobody appreciates the truth of Woodrow Wilson's statement more than John D. Rockefeller, Jr. Back in 1915,

Rockefeller was the most fiercely despised man in Colorado. One of the bloodiest strikes in the history of American industry had been shocking the state for two terrible years. Irate, belligerent miners were demanding higher wages from the Colorado Fuel & Iron Company; and Rockefeller controlled that company. Property had been destroyed, troops had been called out. Blood had been shed. Strikers had been shot, their bodies riddled with bullets.

At a time like that, with the air seething with hatred, Rockefeller wanted to win the strikers to his way of thinking. And he did it. How? Here's the story. After weeks spent in making friends, Rockefeller addressed the representatives of the strikers. This speech, in its entirety, is a masterpiece. It produced astonishing results. It calmed the tempestuous waves of hate that threatened to engulf Rockefeller. It won him a host of admirers. It presented facts in such a friendly manner that the strikers went back to work without saying another word about the increase in wages for which they had fought so violently.

Here is the opening of that remarkable speech. Note how it fairly glows with friendliness.

Remember Rockefeller is talking to men who, a few days previously, wanted to hang him by the neck to a sour apple tree; yet he couldn't have been more gracious, more friendly if he had addressed a group of medical missionaries. His speech is radiant with such phrases as I am *proud* to be here, having *visited* in *your homes*, met many of your wives and children, we meet here not as strangers, but as *friends*, spirit of *mutual friendship*, our *common interests*, it is only by your courtesy that I am here.

"This is a red-letter day in my life," Rockefeller began. "It is the first time I have ever had the good fortune to meet the representatives of the employees of this great company, its officers and superintendents, together, and I can assure you that I am proud to be here, and that I shall remember this gathering as long as I live. Had this meeting been held two weeks ago, I should have stood here a stranger to most of you, recognizing a few faces. Having had the opportunity last week of visiting all the camps in the southern coal fields and of talking individually with

ractically all of the representatives, except those who were
away; having visited in your homes, met many of your
wives and children, we meet here not as strangers, but as
friends, and it is in that spirit of mutual friendship that I
am glad to have this opportunity to discuss with you our
common interests.

"Since this is a meeting of the officers of the company
and the representatives of the employees, it is only by your
courtesy that I am here, for I am not so fortunate as to be
either one or the other; and yet I feel that I am intimately
associated with you men, for, in a sense, I represent both
the stockholders and the directors."

Isn't that a superb example of the fine art of making
friends out of enemies?

Suppose Rockefeller had taken a different tack. Suppose
he had argued with those miners and hurled devastating
facts in their faces. Suppose he had told them by his tones
and insinuations that they were wrong. Suppose that, by
all the rules of logic, he had proved that they were wrong?
What would have happened? More anger would have stirred up, more hatred, more revolt.

*If a man's heart is rankling with discord and ill feeling
toward you, you can't win him to your way of thinking with
all the logic in Christendom. Scolding parents and dom-
ineering bosses and husbands and nagging wives ought to
realize that people don't want to change their minds. They
can't be forced or driven to agree with you or me. But they
may possibly be led to, if we are gentle and friendly, ever
so gentle and ever so friendly.*

Lincoln said that, in effect, almost a hundred years ago.
Here are his words:—

*It is an old and true maxim "that a drop of honey
catches more flies than a gallon of gall." So with men, if
you would win a man to your cause, first convince him
that you are his sincere friend. Therein is a drop of
honey that catches his heart; which, say what you will,
is the great high road to his reason.*

Business men are learning that it pays to be friendly to strikers. For example, when two thousand five hundred employees in the White Motor Company's plant struck for higher wages and a union shop, Robert F. Black, the president, didn't wax wroth and condemn, and threaten and talk of tyranny and Communists. He actually praised the strikers. He published an advertisement in the Cleveland papers, complimenting them on "the peaceful way in which they laid down their tools." Finding the strike pickets idle, he bought them a couple of dozen baseball bats and gloves and invited them to play ball on vacant lots. For those who preferred bowling, he rented a bowling alley.

This friendliness on President Black's part did what friendliness always does: it begot friendliness. So the strikers borrowed brooms, shovels, and rubbish carts, and began picking up matches, papers, cigarette stubs, and cigar butts around the factory. Imagine it! Imagine strikers tidying up the factory grounds while battling for higher wages and recognition of the union. Such an event had never been heard of before in the long, tempestuous history of American labor wars. That strike ended with a compromise settlement within a week—ended without any ill feeling or rancor.

Daniel Webster, who looked like a god and talked like Jehovah, was one of the most successful advocates who ever pleaded a cause; yet he ushered in his most powerful arguments with such friendly remarks as: "It will be for the jury to consider," "This may, perhaps, be worth thinking of, gentlemen," "Here are some facts that I trust you will not lose sight of, gentlemen," or "You, with your knowledge of human nature, will easily see the significance of these facts." No bulldozing. No high-pressure methods. No attempt to force his opinions on other men. Webster used the soft-spoken, quiet, friendly approach, and it helped to make him famous.

You may never be called upon to settle a strike or address a jury, but you may want to get your rent reduced. Will the friendly approach help you then? Let's see.

O. L. Straub, an engineer, wanted to get his rent reduced.

And he knew his landlord was hard-boiled. "I wrote him," Mr. Straub said in a speech before the class, "notifying him that I was vacating my apartment as soon as my lease expired. The truth was I didn't want to move. I wanted to stay if I could get my rent reduced. But the situation seemed hopeless. Other tenants had tried—and failed. Everyone told me that the landlord was extremely difficult to deal with. But I said to myself, 'I am studying a course in how to deal with people, so I'll try it on him—and see how it works.'

"He and his secretary came to see me as soon as he got my letter. I met him at the door with a regular Charlie Schwab greeting. I fairly bubbled with good will and enthusiasm. I didn't begin talking about how high the rent was. I began talking about how much I liked his apartment house. Believe me, I was 'hearty in my approbation and lavish in my praise.' I complimented him on the way he ran the building, and told him I should like so much to stay for another year but I couldn't afford it.

"He had evidently never had such a reception from a tenant. He hardly knew what to make of it.

"Then he started to tell me his troubles. Complaining tenants. One had written him fourteen letters, some of them positively insulting. Another threatened to break his lease unless the landlord kept the man on the floor above from snoring. 'What a relief it is,' he said, 'to have a satisfied tenant like you.' And then without my even asking him to do it, he offered to reduce my rent a little. I wanted more, so I named the figure I could afford to pay, and he accepted without a word.

"As he was leaving, he turned to me and asked, 'What decorating can I have done for you?'

"If I had tried to get the rent reduced by the methods the other tenants were using, I am positive I should have met with the same failure they encountered. It was the friendly, sympathetic, appreciative approach that won."

Let's take another illustration. We'll take a woman this time—a woman from the Social Register—Mrs. Dorothy Day of Garden City on the sandy stretches of Long Island.

"I recently gave a luncheon to a small group of friends," said Mrs. Day. "It was an important occasion for me. Naturally, I was most eager to have everything go off smoothly. Emil, the *maître d'hôtel*, is usually my able assistant in these matters. But on this occasion he let me down. The luncheon was a failure. Emil was nowhere to be seen. He sent only one waiter to take care of us. This waiter hadn't the faintest conception of first-class service. He persisted in serving my guest of honor last. Once he served her one miserable little piece of celery on a large dish. The meat was tough; the potatoes greasy. It was horrible. I was furious. With considerable effort, I smiled through the ordeal, but I kept saying to myself, 'Just wait until I see Emil. I'll give him a piece of my mind all right.'

"This happened on a Wednesday. The next night I heard a lecture on human relationships. As I listened, I realized how futile it would be to give Emil a dressing down. It would make him sullen and resentful. It would kill all desire to help me in the future. I tried to look at it from his standpoint. He hadn't bought the food. He hadn't cooked it. He couldn't help it because some of his waiters were dumb. Perhaps I had been too severe, too hasty in my wrath. So, instead of criticizing him, I decided to begin in a friendly way. I decided to open up on him with appreciation. This approach worked beautifully. I saw Emil the following day. He was defensively angry and spoiling for battle. I said, 'See here, Emil, I want you to know that it means a great deal to me to have you at my back when I entertain. You are the best *maître d'hôtel* in New York. Of course, I fully appreciate that you don't buy the food and cook it. You couldn't help what happened on Wednesday.'

"The clouds disappeared. Emil smiled, and said, 'Exactly, Madam. The trouble was in the kitchen. It was not my fault.'

"So I continued: 'I have planned other parties, Emil, and I need your advice. Do you think we had better give the kitchen another chance?'

" 'Oh, certainly, Madam, of course. It might never happen again.'

"The following week I gave another luncheon. Emil and

I planned the menu. I cut his tip in half, and never mentioned past mistakes.

"When we arrived, the table was colorful with two dozen American beauty roses. Emil was in constant attendance. He could hardly have showered my party with more attention if I had been entertaining Queen Mary. The food was excellent and hot. The service was perfection. The *entrée* was served by four waiters instead of one. Emil personally served delicious mints to finish it off.

"As we were leaving, my guest of honor asked: 'Have you charmed that *maître d'hôtel?* I never saw such service, such attention.'

"She was right. I had charmed with the friendly approach and sincere appreciation."

Years ago, when I was a barefooted boy walking through the woods to a country school out in northwest Missouri, I read a fable one day about the sun and the wind. They quarreled about which was the stronger and the wind said, "I'll prove I am. See the old man down there with a coat? I bet I can make him take his coat off quicker than you can."

So the sun went behind a cloud and the wind blew until it was almost a tornado, but the harder it blew the tighter the old man wrapped his coat about him.

Finally, the wind calmed down and gave up; and then the sun came out from behind the cloud and smiled kindly on the old man. Presently, he mopped his brow and pulled off his coat. The sun then told the wind that gentleness and friendliness were always stronger than fury and force.

Even while I was a boy reading this fable, the truth of it was actually being demonstrated in the far-off town of Boston, an historic center of education and culture that I never dreamed of ever living to see. It was being demonstrated in Boston by Dr. A. H. B——, a physician, who thirty years later became one of my students. Here is the story as Dr. B—— related it in one of his talks before the class:

The Boston newspapers in those days screamed with fake medical advertising—the ads of professional abortionists and quack physicians who pretended to treat the diseases of men and women but who really preyed upon many innocent victims by frightening them with talk about "loss of manhood" or other terrible conditions. Their treatment consisted in keeping the victim filled with terror and in giving him no useful treatment at all. The abortionists had caused many deaths, but there were few convictions. Most paid small fines or got off through political influence.

The condition became so terrible that the good people of Boston rose up in holy indignation. Preachers pounded their pulpits, condemned the papers, and implored the help of Almighty God to stop this advertising. Civic organizations, business men, women's clubs, churches, young people's societies, damned and denounced—all in vain. A bitter fight was waged in the state legislature to make this disgraceful advertising illegal, but it was defeated by graft and political influence.

Dr. B—— was then chairman of the Good Citizenship Committee of the Greater Boston Christian Endeavor Union. His committee had tried everything. It had failed. The fight against these medical criminals seemed hopeless.

Then one night, after midnight, Dr. B—— tried something that apparently no one in Boston had ever thought of trying before. He tried kindness, sympathy, appreciation. He tried to make the publishers actually *want* to stop the advertising. He wrote the publisher of *The Boston Herald,* telling him how much he admired his paper. He had always read it; the news items were clean, not sensational; and the editorials were excellent. It was a splendid family paper. Dr. B—— declared that it was, in his opinion, the best paper in New England and one of the finest in America. "But," continued Dr. B——, "a friend of mine has a young daughter. He told me his daughter read one of your advertisements aloud to him the other night, the advertisement of a professional abortionist, and then asked him what was meant by some of the phrases. Frankly, he was embarrassed. He didn't know what to say. Your paper goes into the best homes in Boston. If that happened in the home of my friend, isn't it probable that it is happening in many other homes also? If you had a young daughter, would you want her to read those advertisements? And if she did read them and ask you about them, how could you explain?

"I am sorry that such a splendid paper as yours—almost perfect in every other way—has this one feature which makes some fathers dread to see their daughters pick it up. Isn't it probable that thousands of your other subscribers feel about it just as I do?"

Two days later the publisher of *The Boston Herald* wrote Dr. B——; the doctor kept the letter in his files for a third of a century and gave it to me when he was a member of my course. I have it in front of me now as I write. It is dated October 13, 1904.

A. H. B.——, M.D.
Boston, Mass.

Dear Sir:
I really feel under obligations to you for your letter of the 11th inst., addressed to the editor of this paper, inasmuch as it has finally decided me on an action which I have had under contemplation ever since I have been in charge here.

Beginning Monday, I propose to have *The Boston Herald* absolutely expurgated of all objectionable advertising matter, as far as it is possible to do so. The medical cards, the whirling spray syringe, and like advertising, will be absolutely "killed," and all other medical advertising, which it is impossible to keep out at this time will be so thoroughly edited that it will be absolutely inoffensive.

Again thanking you for your kind letter, which has been helpful in this respect, I beg to remain,

Yours sincerely,
W. E. Haskell,
Publisher.

Aesop was a Greek slave who lived at the court of Croesus and spun immortal fables six hundred years before Christ. Yet the truths he taught about human nature are just as true in Boston and Birmingham now as they were twenty-five centuries ago in Athens. The sun can make you take off your coat more quickly than the wind; and kindliness, the friendly approach, and appreciation can make people change their minds more readily than all the bluster and storming in Christendom.

Remember what Lincoln said: "A drop of honey catches more flies than a gallon of gall."

When you wish to win people to your way of thinking, don't forget to use **Rule 4**:

Begin in a friendly way.

CHAPTER FIVE

The Secret of Socrates

IN TALKING WITH PEOPLE, don't begin by discussing the things on which you differ. Begin by emphasizing—and keep on emphasizing—the things on which you agree. Keep emphasizing—if possible—that you are both striving for the same end and your only difference is one of method and not of purpose.

Get the other person saying, "Yes, yes," at the outset. Keep him, if possible, from saying "No."

"A 'No' response," says Professor Overstreet in his book, *Influencing Human Behavior,* "is a most difficult handicap to overcome. When a person has said 'No,' all his pride of personality demands that he remain consistent with himself. He may later feel that the 'No' was ill-advised; nevertheless, there is his precious pride to consider! Once having said a thing, he must stick to it. Hence it is of the very greatest importance that we start a person in the affirmative direction."

The skillful speaker gets "at the outset a number of 'yes responses.' He has thereby set the psychological processes of his listeners moving in the affirmative direction. It is like the movement of a billiard ball. Propel it in one direction, and it takes some force to deflect it; far more force to send it back in the opposite direction.

"The psychological patterns here are quite clear. When a person says 'No' and really means it, he is doing far more than saying a word of two letters. His entire organism—glandular, nervous, muscular—gathers itself together into a condition of rejection. There is, usually in minute but sometimes in observable degree, a physical withdrawal, or readiness for withdrawal. The whole neuro-muscular system, in short, sets itself on guard against acceptance. Where, on the contrary, a person says 'Yes,' none of the withdrawing activities take place. The organism is in a forward-moving, accepting, open attitude. Hence the more 'Yeses' we can, at the very outset, induce, the more likely we are to succeed in capturing the attention for our ultimate proposal.

"It is a very simple technique—this yes response. And yet how much neglected! It often seems as if people get a sense of their own importance by antagonizing at the outset. The radical comes into a conference with his conservative brethren; and immediately he must make them furious! What, as a matter of fact, is the good of it? If he simply does it in order to get some pleasure out of it for himself, he may be pardoned. But if he expects to achieve something, he is only psychologically stupid.

"Get a student to say 'No' at the beginning, or a customer, child, husband, or wife, and it takes the wisdom and the patience of angels to transform that bristling negative into an affirmative."

The use of his "yes, yes" technique enabled James Eberson, teller for the Greenwich Savings Bank, New York City, to save a prospective customer who might otherwise have been lost.

"This man came in to open an account," said Mr. Eberson, "and I gave him our usual form to fill out. Some of the questions he answered willingly, but there were others he flatly refused to answer.

"Before I began the study of human relations, I should have told this prospective depositor that if he refused to give the bank this information, we should have to refuse to accept his account. I am ashamed that I have been guilty of doing that very thing in the past. Naturally, an ultimatum like that made me feel good. I had shown who was boss, that the bank's rules and regulations couldn't be flouted. But that sort of an attitude certainly didn't give a feeling of welcome and importance to the man who had walked in to give us his patronage.

"I resolved this morning to use a little horse sense. I resolved not to talk about what the bank wanted but about what the customer wanted. And above all else, I was determined to get him saying 'yes, yes' from the very start. So I agreed with him. I told him the information he refused to give was not absolutely necessary.

" 'However,' I said, 'suppose you have money in this bank at your death. Wouldn't you like to have the bank transfer it to your next of kin who is entitled to it according to law?'

" 'Yes, of course,' he replied.

" 'Don't you think,' I continued, 'that it would be a good idea to give us the name of your next of kin so that, in the event of your death, we could carry out your wishes without error or delay?'

"Again he said, 'Yes.'

"The young man's attitude softened and changed when he realized that we weren't asking for this information for our sake but for his sake. Before leaving the bank, this young man not only gave me complete information about himself but he opened, at my suggestion, a trust account naming his mother as the beneficiary for his account and he gladly answered all the questions concerning his mother also.

"I found that by getting him saying 'yes, yes' from the outset, he forgot the issue at stake and was happy to do all the things I suggested."

"There was a man on my territory that our company was most eager to sell," said Joseph Allison, salesman for Westinghouse. "My predecessor had called on him for ten years without selling anything. When I took over the territory, I called steadily for three years without getting an order. Finally, after thirteen years of calls and sales talk, we sold him a few motors. If these proved to be all right, I felt sure of an order for several hundred more. Such was my expectation.

"Right? I knew they would be all right. So when I called three weeks later, I was stepping high."

"But I didn't step high very long for the chief engineer greeted me with this shocking announcement: 'Allison, I can't buy the remainder of the motors from you.'

" 'Why?' I asked in amazement. 'Why?'

" 'Because your motors are too hot. I can't put my hand on them.'

"I knew it wouldn't do any good to argue. I had tried that sort of thing too long. So I thought of getting the 'yes, yes' response.

" 'Well, now look, Mr. Smith,' I said. 'I agree with you a hundred per cent; if those motors are running too hot, you ought not to buy any more of them. You must have motors that won't run any hotter than standards set by the regulations of the National Electrical Manufacturers' Association. Isn't that so?"

"He agreed it was. I had gotten my first 'yes.'

" 'The Electrical Manufacturers' Association regulations say that a properly designed motor may have a temperature of 72 degrees Fahrenheit above room temperature. Is that correct?'

" 'Yes,' he agreed. 'That's quite correct. But your motors are much hotter.'

"I didn't argue with him. I merely asked: 'How hot is the mill room?'

" 'Oh.' he said, 'about 75 degrees Fahrenheit.'

" 'Well,' I replied, 'if the mill room is 75 degrees and you add 72 to that, that makes a total of 147 degrees Fahrenheit. Wouldn't you scald your hand if you held it under a spigot of hot water at a temperature of 147 degrees Fahrenheit?'

"Again he had to say yes.

" 'Well.' I suggested, 'wouldn't it be a good idea to keep your hands off those motors?'

" 'Well, I guess you're right,' he admitted. We continued

to chat for awhile. Then he called his secretary and lined up approximately $35,000 worth of business for the ensuing month.

"It took me years and cost me countless thousands of dollars in lost business before I finally learned that it doesn't pay to argue, that it is much more profitable and much more interesting to look at things from the other man's viewpoint and try to get him saying 'yes, yes.' "

Socrates, "the gadfly of Athens," was a brilliant old boy in spite of the fact that he went barefooted and married a girl of nineteen when he was bald-headed and forty. He did something that only a handful of men in all history have been able to do: he sharply changed the whole course of human thought; and now, twenty-three centuries after his death, he is honored as one of the wisest persuaders who ever influenced this wrangling world.

His method? Did he tell people they were wrong? Oh, no, not Socrates. He was far too adroit for that. His whole technique, now called the "Socratic method," was based upon getting a "yes, yes" response. He asked questions with which his opponent would have to agree. He kept on winning one admission after another until he had an armful of yeses. He kept on asking questions until finally, almost without realizing it, his opponent found himself embracing a conclusion that he would have bitterly denied a few minutes previously.

The next time we are smarting to tell a man he is wrong, let's remember barefooted old Socrates and ask a gentle question—a question that will get the "yes, yes" response.

The Chinese have a proverb pregnant with the age-old wisdom of the changeless East: "He who treads softly goes far."

They have spent five thousand years studying human nature, those cultured Chinese, and they have garnered a lot of perspicacity: "He who treads softly goes far."

If you want to win people to your way of thinking, Rule 5 is:

Get the other person saying "yes, yes" immediately.

CHAPTER SIX

The Safety Valve
in Handling Complaints

MOST PEOPLE, when trying to win others to their way of thinking, do too much talking themselves. Salesmen, especially, are guilty of this costly error. Let the other man talk himself out. He knows more about his business and his problems than you do. So ask him questions. Let him tell you a few things.

If you disagree with him, you may be tempted to interrupt. But don't. It is dangerous. He won't pay attention to you while he still has a lot of ideas of his own crying for expression. So listen patiently and with an open mind. Be sincere about it. Encourage him to express his ideas fully.

Does this policy pay in business? Let's see. Here is the story of a man who was *forced* to try it.

A few years ago, one of the largest automobile manufacturers in the United States was negotiating for a year's requirements of upholstery fabrics. Three important manufacturers had worked up fabrics in sample bodies. These had all been inspected by the executives of the motor company, and notice had been sent to each manufacturer saying that, on a certain day, his representative would be given an opportunity of making his final plea for the contract.

G. B. R., a representative of one manufacturer, arrived in town with a severe attack of laryngitis. "When it came my turn to meet the executives in conference," Mr. R. said as he related the story before one of my classes, "I had lost my voice. I could hardly whisper. I was ushered into a room and found myself face to face with the textile engineer, the purchasing agent, the director of sales, and the president of the company. I stood up and made a valiant effort to speak, but I couldn't do anything more than squeak.

"They were all seated around a table, so I wrote on a pad of paper: 'Gentlemen, I have lost my voice. I am speechless.'

" 'I'll do the talking for you,' the president said. He did. He exhibited my samples and praised their good points. A lively discussion arose about the merits of my goods. And the president, since he was talking for me, took my side during the discussion. My sole participation consisted of smiles, nods, and a few gestures.

"As a result of this unique conference, I was awarded the contract, which called for over half a million yards of upholstery fabrics at an aggregate value of $1,600,000— the biggest order I ever received.

"I know I should have lost that contract if I hadn't lost my voice, because I had the wrong idea about the whole proposition. I discovered, quite by accident, how richly it sometimes pays to let the other fellow do the talking."

Joseph S. Webb of the Philadelphia Electric Company made the same discovery. Mr. Webb was making a rural inspection trip through a district of prosperous Pennsylvania Dutch farmers.

"Why aren't those people using electricity?" he asked the district representative as they passed a well-kept farmhouse.

"They're tightwads. You can't sell them anything," the district man answered in disgust. "And, besides, they're sore at the company. I've tried. It's hopeless."

Maybe it was, but Webb decided to try anyway, so he

knocked at the farmhouse door. The door opened by a narrow crack, and old Mrs. Druckenbrod peered out.

"As soon as she saw the company representative," said Mr. Webb, as he related the story, "she slammed the door in our faces. I knocked again, and again she opened the door; and this time she began to tell us what she thought of us and our company.

" 'Mrs. Druckenbrod,' I said, 'I'm sorry we've troubled you. But I didn't come here to sell you electricity. I merely wanted to buy some eggs.'"

"She opened the door wider and peered out at us suspiciously.

" 'I noticed your fine flock of Dominicks,' I said, 'and I should like to buy a dozen fresh eggs.'

"The door opened a little wider. 'How'd you know my hens were Dominicks?' she inquired, her curiosity piqued.

" 'I raise chickens myself,' I replied. 'And I must say, I've never seen a finer flock of Dominicks.'

" 'Why don't you use your own eggs then?' she demanded, still somewhat suspicious.

" 'Because my Leghorns lay white eggs. And naturally, being a cook myself, you know white eggs can't compare to brown eggs when it comes to making cake. And my wife prides herself on her cakes.'

"By this time, Mrs. Druckenbrod ventured out onto the porch in a much more amiable frame of mind. Meantime, my eyes had been wandering around and I had discovered that the farm was equipped with a fine-looking dairy.

" 'As a matter of fact, Mrs. Druckenbrod,' I continued, 'I'll bet you make more money from your hens than your husband makes with his dairy.'

"Bang! She was off! Sure she did! And she loved to tell me about it. But, alas, she couldn't make her old husband, the blockhead, admit it.

"She invited us down to see her poultry house; and on our tour of inspection I noticed various little contraptions that she had built, and I was 'hearty in my approbation and lavish in my praise.' I recommended certain feeds and certain temperatures; and asked her advice on several points;

and soon we were having a good time swapping experiences.

"Presently, she remarked that some of her neighbors had put electric lights in their hen houses and they claimed they had got excellent results. She wanted my honest opinion as to whether or not it would pay her to do the same thing . . .

"Two weeks later, Mr. Druckenbrod's Dominick hens were clucking and scratching contentedly in the encouraging glow of electric lights. I had my order; she was getting more eggs; everyone was satisfied; everyone had gained.

"But—and this is the point of the story—I should never have sold electricity to this Pennsylvania Dutch farmwife, if I had not first let her talk herself into it!

"Such people can't be sold. You have to let them buy."

A large advertisement appeared recently on the financial page of the *New York Herald Tribune* calling for a man with unusual ability and experience. Charles T. Cubellis answered the advertisement, sending his reply to a box number. A few days later, he was invited by letter to call for an interview. Before he called, he spent hours in Wall Street finding out everything possible about the man who had founded the business. During the interview, he remarked: "I should be mighty proud to be associated with an organization with a record like yours. I understand you started twenty-eight years ago with nothing but desk room and one stenographer. Is that true?"

Almost every successful man likes to reminisce about his early struggles. This man was no exception. He talked for a long time about how he had started with four hundred and fifty dollars in cash and an original idea. He told how he had fought against discouragement and battled against ridicule, working Sundays and holidays, twelve to sixteen hours a day; how he had finally won against all odds until now the biggest men in Wall Street were coming to him for information and guidance. He was proud of such a record. He had a right to be, and he had a splendid time telling about it. Finally, he questioned Mr. Cubellis briefly about his experience, then called in one of his vice presidents and said: "I think this is the man we are looking for."

Mr. Cubellis had taken the trouble to find out about the accomplishments of his prospective employer. He showed an interest in the other man and his problems. He encouraged the other man to do most of the talking—and made a favorable impression.

The truth is that even our friends would far rather talk to us about their achievements than listen to us boast about ours.

La Rochefoucauld, the French philosopher, said: "If you want enemies, excel your friends; but if you want friends, let your friends excel you."

Why is that true? Because when our friends excel us, that gives them a feeling of importance; but when we excel them, that gives them a feeling of inferiority and arouses envy and jealousy.

The Germans have a proverb: "Die reinste Freude ist die Schadenfreude," which, being interpreted, goes something like this: "The purest joy is the malicious joy we take in the misfortunes of those we have envied." Or, to put it another way: "The purest joy is the joy we take in other people's troubles."

Yes, some of your friends probably get more satisfaction out of your troubles than out of your triumphs.

So, let's minimize our achievements. Let's be modest. That always makes a hit. Irvin Cobb had the right technique. A lawyer once said to Cobb on the witness stand: "I understand, Mr. Cobb, that you are one of the most famous writers in America. Is that correct?"

"I have probably been more fortunate than I deserve," Cobb replied.

We ought to be modest, for neither you nor I amount to much. Both of us will pass on and be completely forgotten a century from now. Life is too short to bore other people with talk of our petty accomplishments. Let's encourage them to talk instead. Come to think about it, you haven't much to brag about anyhow. Do you know what keeps you from becoming an idiot? Not much. Only a nickel's worth of iodine in your thyroid glands. If a physician were to open the thyroid gland in your neck and take out a little iodine, you would become an idiot. A little iodine that can be bought at a corner drugstore for five cents is all that stands between you and an institution for the mentally ill. A nickel's worth of iodine! That isn't much to be boasting about, is it?

So, if we want to win people to our way of thinking, **Rule 6** is:

Let the other man do a great deal of the talking.

How to Get Co-operation

DON'T YOU HAVE much more faith in ideas that you discover for yourself than in ideas that are handed to you on a silver platter? If so, isn't it bad judgment to try to ram your opinions down the throats of other people? Wouldn't it be wiser to make suggestions—and let the other man think out the conclusion for himself?

To illustrate: Mr. Adolph Seltz of Philadelphia, a student of one of my courses, suddenly found himself confronted with the necessity of injecting enthusiasm into a discouraged and disorganized group of automobile salesmen. Calling a sales meeting, he urged his men to tell him exactly what they expected from him. As they talked, he wrote their ideas on the blackboard. He then said: "I'll give you all these qualities you expect from me. Now I want you to tell me what I have a right to expect from you." The replies came quick and fast: loyalty, honesty, initiative, optimism, team work, eight hours a day of enthusiastic work. One man volunteered to work fourteen hours a day. The meeting ended with a new courage, a new inspiration, and Mr. Seltz reported to me that the increase of sales had been phenomenal.

"The men had made a sort of moral bargain with me," said Mr. Seltz, "and as long as I lived up to my part in it, they were determined to live up to theirs. Consulting them about their wishes and desires was just the shot in the arm they needed."

No man likes to feel that he is being sold something or told to do a thing. We much prefer to feel that we are buying of our own accord or acting on our own ideas. We like to be consulted about our wishes, our wants, our thoughts.

For example, take the case of Eugene Wesson. He lost countless thousands of dollars in commissions before he learned this truth. Mr. Wesson sells sketches for a studio that creates designs for stylists and textile manufacturers. Mr. Wesson had called once a week, every week for three years, on one of the leading stylists in New York. "He never refused to see me," said Mr. Wesson, "but he never bought. He always looked over my sketches very carefully and then said: 'No, Wesson, I guess we don't get together today.'"

After a hundred and fifty failures, Wesson realized he must be in a mental rut; so he resolved to devote one evening a week to the study of influencing human behavior, and to develop new ideas and generate new enthusiasms.

Presently he was stimulated to try a new approach. Picking up half a dozen unfinished sketches the artists were working on, he rushed over to his buyer's office. "I want you to do me a little favor, if you will," he said. "Here are some uncompleted sketches. Won't you please tell me how we could finish them up in such a way that they would be of service to you?"

The buyer looked at the sketches for a while without uttering a word and then said: "Leave these with me for a few days, Wesson, and then come back and see me."

Wesson returned three days later, got his suggestions, took the sketches back to the studio and had them finished according to the buyer's ideas. The result? All accepted.

That was nine months ago. Since that time, this buyer has ordered scores of other sketches, all drawn according to his ideas—and the net result has been more than sixteen hundred dollars in commisions for Wesson. "I now realize why I failed for years to sell his buyer," said Wesson. "I had urged him to buy what I thought he ought to have. I do the very opposite now. I urge him to give me his ideas. He feels now that he is creating the designs. And he is. I don't have to sell him now. He buys."

When Theodore Roosevelt was Governor of New York, he accomplished an extraordinary feat. He kept on good terms with the political bosses and yet he forced through reforms which they bitterly disliked. And here is how he did it.

When an important office was to be filled, he invited the political bosses to make recommendations. "At first," said Roosevelt, "they might propose a broken-down party hack, the sort of man who has to be 'taken care of.' I would tell them that to appoint such a man would not be good politics, as the public would not approve it.

"Then they would bring me the name of another party hack, a persistent office holder, who, if he had nothing against him, had little in his favor. I would tell them that this man would not measure up to the expectations of the public, and I would ask them to see if they could not find someone more obviously fitted for the post.

"Their third suggestion would be a man who was almost good enough, but not quite.

"Then I would thank them, asking them to try once more, and their fourth suggestion would be acceptable; they would then name just the sort of man I should have picked out myself. Expressing my gratitude for their assistance, I would appoint this man—*and I would let them take the credit for the appointment*. . . . I would tell them that I had done these things to please them and now it was their turn to please me."

And they did. They did it by supporting such sweeping reforms as the Civil Service Bill and the Franchise Tax Bill.

Remember, Roosevelt went to great lengths to consult the other man and show respect for his advice. When Roosevelt made an important appointment, he let the bosses really feel that they had selected the candidate, that the idea was theirs.

An automobile dealer on Long Island used this same technique to sell a used car to a Scotsman and his wife. This dealer had shown the Scotsman car after car, but there was always something wrong. This didn't suit. That was out of kilter. The price was too high. Always the price was too high. At this juncture, the dealer, a member of one of my courses, appealed to the class for help.

We advised him to quit trying to sell "Sandy" and let "Sandy" buy. We said, instead of telling "Sandy" what to do, why not let him tell you what to do? Let him feel that the idea is his.

That sounded good. So the dealer tried it a few days later when a customer wanted to trade an old car in on a new one. The dealer knew this used car might appeal to "Sandy." So, he picked up the phone and asked "Sandy" if he wouldn't, as a special favor, come over and give him a bit of advice.

When "Sandy" arrived, the dealer said: "You are a shrewd buyer. You know car values. Won't you please look over this car and try it out and tell me how much I ought to allow for it in a trade?"

"Sandy" was "one vast substantial smile." At last his advice was being sought, his ability was being recognized. He drove the car up Queens Boulevard from Jamaica to Forest Hills and back again. "If you can get that car for three hundred," he advised, "you'll be getting a bargain."

"If I can get it at that figure, would you be willing to buy it?" the dealer inquired. Three hundred? Of course. That was his idea, his appraisal. The deal was closed immediately.

The same psychology was used by an X-ray manufacturer to sell his equipment to one of the largest hospitals in Brooklyn. This hospital was building an addition, and preparing to equip it with the finest X-ray department in America. Dr. L——, who was in charge of the X-ray department, was overwhelmed with salesmen, each caroling the praises of his own equipment.

One manufacturer, however, was more skillful. He knew far more about handling human nature than the others did. He wrote a letter something like this:

> Our factory has recently completed a new line of X-ray equipment. The first shipment of these machines has just arrived at our office. They are not perfect. We know that, and we want to improve them. So we should be deeply obligated to you if you could find time to look them over and give us your ideas about how they can be made more serviceable to your profession. Knowing how occupied you are, I shall be glad to send my car for you at any hour you specify.

"I was surprised to get that letter," Dr. L——said, as he related the incident before the class. "I was both surprised and complimented. I had never had an X-ray manufacturer seeking my advice before. It made me feel important. I was busy every night that week, but I canceled a dinner appointment in order to look over that equipment. The more I studied it, the more I discovered for myself how much I liked it.

"Nobody had tried to sell it to me. I felt that the idea of buying that equipment for the hospital was my own. I sold myself on its superior qualities and ordered it installed."

Colonel Edward M. House wielded an enormous influence in national and international affairs while Woodrow Wilson occupied the White House. Wilson leaned upon Colonel House for secret counsel and advice more than he did upon even members of his own cabinet.

What method did the Colonel use in influencing the President? Fortunately we know, for House himself revealed it to Arthur D. Howden Smith, and Smith quoted House in an article in *The Saturday Evening Post*.

"'After I got to know the President,' House said, 'I learned the best way to convert him to an idea was to plant it in his mind casually, but so as to interest him in it—so as to get him thinking about it on his own account. The first time this worked it was an accident. I had been visiting him at the White House, and urged a policy on him which he appeared to disapprove. But several days later, at the dinner table, I was amazed to hear him trot out my suggestion as his own.'"

Did House interrupt him and say, "That's not your idea. That's mine?" Oh, no. Not House. He was too adroit for that. He didn't care about credit. He wanted results. So he let Wilson continue to feel that the idea was his. House did even more than that. He gave Wilson public credit for these ideas.

Let's remember that the people with whom we come in contact tomorrow will be just as human as Woodrow Wilson. So let's use the technique of Colonel House.

A man up in New Brunswick used this technique on me a few years ago—and got my patronage. I was planning at the time to do some fishing and canoeing in New Brunswick. So I wrote the tourist bureau for information. My name and address were evidently put on a public list, for I was immediately overwhelmed with scores of letters and booklets and printed testimonials from camps and guides. I was bewildered. I didn't know which to choose. Then one camp owner did a very clever thing. He sent me the names and telephone numbers of several New York people he had served and invited me to telephone them and discover for myself what he had to offer.

I found to my surprise that I knew one of the men on his list. I telephoned him, found out what his experiences had been, and then wired the camp the date of my arrival.

The others had been trying to sell me on their service, but one chap let me sell myself. He won.

So if you want to influence people to your way of thinking, **Rule 7** is:

Let the other fellow feel that the idea is his.

Twenty-five centuries ago, Lao-tse, a Chinese sage, said some things that readers of this book might use today:

"The reason why rivers and seas receive the homage of a hundred mountain streams is that they keep below them. Thus they are able to reign over all the mountain streams. So the sage, wishing to be above men, putteth himself below them; wishing to be before them, he putteth himself behind them. Thus, though his place be above men, they do not feel his weight; though his place be before them, they do not count it an injury."

CHAPTER EIGHT

A Formula That Will Work Wonders For You

REMEMBER that the other man may be totally wrong. But he doesn't think so. Don't condemn him. Any fool can do that. Try to understand him. Only wise, tolerant, exceptional men even try to do that.

There is a reason why the other man thinks and acts as he does. Ferret out that hidden reason—and you have the key to his actions, perhaps to his personality.

Try honestly to put yourself in his place.

If you say to yourself, "How would I feel, how would I react if I were in his shoes?" you will save a lot of time and irritation, for "by becoming interested in the cause, we are less likely to dislike the effect." And, in addition, you will sharply increase your skill in human relationships.

"Stop a minute," says Kenneth M. Goode, in his book, *How to Turn People into Gold*, "stop a minute to contrast your keen interest in your own affairs with your mild concern about anything else. Realize then, that everybody else in the world feels exactly the same way! Then, along with

Lincoln and Roosevelt, you will have grasped the only solid foundation for any job other than warden in a penitentiary: namely, that success in dealing with people depends on a sympathetic grasp of the other man's viewpoint."

For years, I have taken a great deal of my recreation by walking and riding in a park near my home. Like the Druids of ancient Gaul, I all but worship an oak tree, so I was distressed season after season to see the young trees and shrubs killed off by needless fires. These fires weren't caused by careless smokers. They were almost all caused by boys who went out to the park to go native and cook a frankfurter or an egg under the trees. Sometimes, these fires raged so fiercely that the fire department had to be called out to fight the conflagration.

There was a sign on the edge of the park saying that anyone who started a fire was liable to fine and imprisonment; but the sign stood in an unfrequented part of the park and few boys ever saw it. A mounted policeman was supposed to look after the park; but he didn't take his duties too seriously, and the fires continued to spread season after season. On one occasion, I rushed up to a policeman and told him about a fire spreading rapidly through the park and wanted him to notify the fire department; and he nonchalantly replied that it was none of his business because it wasn't in his precinct! I was desperate, so after that when I went riding, I acted as a self-appointed committee of one to protect the public domain. In the beginning, I am afraid I didn't even attempt to see the boys' point of view. When I saw a fire blazing under the trees, I was so unhappy about it, so eager to do the right thing, that I did the wrong thing. I would ride up to the boys, warn them that they could be jailed for starting a fire, order it put out with a tone of authority; and, if they refused, I would threaten to have them arrested. I was merely unloading my feelings without thinking of their point of view.

The result? The boys obeyed—obeyed sullenly and with resentment. After I rode on over the hill, they probably rebuilt the fire; and longed to burn up the whole park.

With the passing of the years, I hope I acquired a trifle more knowledge of human relations, a little more tact, a little greater tendency to see things from the other person's point of view. Then, instead of giving orders, I would ride up to a blazing fire and begin something like this:

Having a good time, boys? What are you going to cook for supper? . . . I loved to build fires myself when I was a boy—and I still love to. But you know they are very dangerous here in the park. I know you boys don't mean to do any harm; but other boys aren't so careful. They come along and see that you have built a fire; so they build one and don't put it out when they go home, and it spreads among the dry leaves and kills the trees. We won't have any trees here at all if we aren't more careful. You could be put in jail for building this fire. But I don't want to be bossy and interfere with your pleasure. I like to see you enjoy yourselves; but won't you please rake all the leaves away from the fire right now—and you'll be careful to cover it with dirt, a lot of dirt, before you leave, won't you? And the next time you want to have some fun, won't you please build your fire over the hill there in the sand pit? It can't do any damage there. . . . Thanks so much boys. Have a good time.

What a difference that kind of talk made! That made the boys want to co-operate. No sullenness, no resentment. They hadn't been forced to obey orders. They had saved their faces. They felt better and I felt better because I had handled the situation with consideration for their point of view.

Tomorrow, before asking anyone to put out a fire or buy a can of Afta cleaning fluid or give fifty dollars to the Red Cross, why not pause and close your eyes and try to think the whole thing through from the other person's point of view? Ask yourself: "Why should he want to do it?" True, that will take time; but it will make friends and get better results and get them with less friction and less shoe leather.

"I should rather walk the sidewalk in front of a man's office for two hours before an interview," said Dean Donham of the Harvard business school, "than step into his office without a perfectly clear idea of what I am going to say and what he—from my knowledge of his interests and motives—is likely to answer."

That is so important that I am going to repeat it in italics for the sake of emphasis.

I should rather walk the sidewalk in front of a man's office for two hours before an interview, than step into his office without a perfectly clear idea of what I am going to say and what he—from my knowledge of his interests and motives—is likely to answer.

If, as a result of reading this book, you get only one thing—an increased tendency to think always in terms of the other person's point of view, and see things from his angle as well as your own—if you get only that one thing from this book, it may easily prove to be one of the milestones of your career.

Therefore, if you want to change people without giving offense or arousing resentment, **Rule 8** is:

Try honestly to see things from the other person's point of view.

CHAPTER NINE

What Everybody Wants

WOULDN'T YOU LIKE to have a magic phrase that would stop argument, eliminate ill feeling, create good will, and make the other person listen attentively?

Yes? All right. Here it is. Begin by saying: "I don't blame you one iota for feeling as you do. If I were you, I should undoubtedly feel just as you do."

An answer like that will soften the most cantankerous old cuss alive. And you can say that and be one hundred per cent sincere, because if you were the other person, of course you would feel just as he does. Let me illustrate. Take Al Capone, for example. Suppose you had inherited the same body and temperament and mind that Al Capone inherited. Suppose you had had his environment and experiences. You would then be precisely what he was—and where he was. For it is those things—and only those things —that made him what he was.

The only reason, for example, that you are not a rattlesnake is that your mother and father weren't rattlesnakes. The only reason you don't kiss cows and consider snakes

166

holy is because you weren't born in a Hindu family on the banks of the Brahmaputra.

You deserve very little credit for being what you are—and remember, the man who comes to you irritated, bigoted, unreasoning, deserves very little discredit for being what he is. Feel sorry for the poor devil. Pity him. Sympathize with him. Say to yourself what John B. Gough used to say when he saw a drunken bum staggering down the street: "There, but for the grace of God, go I."

Three-fourths of the people you will meet tomorrow are hungering and thirsting for sympathy. Give it to them, and they will love you.

I once gave a broadcast about the author of *Little Women*, Louisa May Alcott. Naturally, I knew she had lived and written her immortal books in Concord, Massachusetts. But, without thinking what I was saying, I spoke of visiting her old home in Concord, New Hampshire. If I had said New Hampshire only once, it might have been forgiven. But, alas! alack! I said it twice. I was deluged with letters and telegrams, stinging messages that swirled around my defenseless head like a swarm of hornets. Many were indignant. A few insulting. One Colonial Dame, who had been reared in Concord, Massachusetts, and who was then living in Philadelphia, vented her scorching wrath upon me. She couldn't have been much more bitter if I had accused Miss Alcott of being a cannibal from New Guinea. As I read the letter, I said to myself, "Thank God, I am not married to that girl." I felt like writing and telling her that although I had made a mistake in geography, she had made a far greater mistake in common courtesy. That was to be just my opening sentence. Then I was going to roll up my sleeves and tell her what I really thought. But I didn't. I controlled myself. I realized that any hot-headed fool could do that—and that most fools would do just that.

I wanted to be above fools. So I resolved to try to turn her hostility into friendliness. That would be a challenge, a sort of a game I could play. I said to myself, "After all, if I were she, I should probably feel just as she does." So, I determined to sympathize with her viewpoint. The next time

I was in Philadelphia, I called her on the telephone. The conversation went something like this:

ME: Mrs. So-and-so, you wrote me a letter a few weeks ago, and I want to thank you for it.

SHE *(in incisive, cultured, well-bred tones)*: To whom have I the honor of speaking?

ME: I am a stranger to you. My name is Dale Carnegie. You listened to a broadcast I gave about Louisa May Alcott a few Sundays ago, and I made the unforgivable blunder of saying that she had lived in Concord, New Hampshire. It was a stupid blunder and I want to apologize for it. It was so nice of you to take the time to write me.

SHE: I am sorry, Mr. Carnegie, that I wrote as I did. I lost my temper. I must apologize.

ME: No! No! You are not the one to apologize; I am the one to apologize. Any school child would have known better than to have said what I said. I apologized over the air the Sunday following and I want to apologize to you personally now.

SHE: I was born in Concord, Massachusetts. My family has been prominent in Massachusetts affairs for two centuries and I am very proud of my native state. I was really quite distressed to hear you say that Miss Alcott was born in New Hampshire. But I am really ashamed of that letter.

ME: I assure you that you were not one-tenth as distressed as I am. My error didn't hurt Massachusetts; but it did hurt me. It is so seldom that people of your standing and culture take the time to write people who speak on the radio, and I do hope you will write me again if you detect an error in my talks.

SHE: You know, I really like very much the way you have accepted my criticism. You must be a very nice person. I should like to know you better.

So, by apologizing and sympathizing with her point of view, I got her apologizing and sympathizing with my point of view. I had the satisfaction of controlling my temper, the

satisfaction of returning kindness for an insult. I got infinitely more real fun out of making her like me then I could
ever have gotten out of telling her to go and take a jump in
the Schuylkill River.

Every man who occupies the White House is faced almost daily with thorny problems in human relations. President Taft was no exception, and he learned from experience
the enormous chemical value of sympathy in neutralizing
the acid of hard feelings. In his book, *Ethics in Service,*
Taft gives rather an amusing illustration of how he softened
the ire of a disappointed and ambitious mother.

"A lady in Washington," writes Taft, "whose husband
had some political influence, came and labored with me for
six weeks or more to appoint her son to a position. She
secured the aid of Senators and Congressmen in formidable
number and came with them to see that they spoke with
emphasis. The place was one requiring technical qualifications, and following the recommendation of the head of the
Bureau, I appointed somebody else. I then received a letter
from the mother, saying that I was most ungrateful, since
I declined to make her a happy woman as I could have
done by a turn of my hand. She complained further that
she had labored with her state delegation and got all the
votes for an administration bill in which I was especially
interested and this was the way I had rewarded her.

"When you get a letter like that, the first thing you do is
to think how you can be severe with a person who has committed an impropriety, or even been a little impertinent.
Then you may compose an answer. Then if you are wise,
you will put the letter in a drawer and lock the drawer.
Take it out in the course of two days—such communica-
tions will always bear two days' delay in answering—and
when you take it out after that interval, you will not send it.
That is just the course I took. After that, I sat down and
wrote her just as polite a letter as I could, telling her I
realized a mother's disappointment under such circumstances, but that really the appointment was not left to my
mere personal preference, that I had to select a man with
technical qualifications, and had, therefore, to follow the

recommendations of the head of the Bureau. I expressed the hope that her son would go on to accomplish what she had hoped for him in the position which he then had. That mollified her and she wrote me a note saying she was sorry she had written as she had.

"But the appointment I sent in was not confirmed at once, and after an interval I received a letter which purported to come from her husband, though it was in the same handwriting as all the others. I was therein advised that, due to the nervous prostration that had followed her disappointment in this case, she had to take to her bed and had developed a most serious case of cancer of the stomach. Would I not restore her to health by withdrawing the first name and replacing it by her son's? I had to write another letter, this one to the husband, to say that I hoped the diagnosis would prove to be inaccurate, that I sympathized with him in the sorrow he must have in the serious illness of his wife, but that it was impossible to withdraw the name sent in. The man whom I appointed was confirmed, and within two days after I received that letter, we gave a musicale at the White House. The first two people to greet Mrs. Taft and me were this husband and wife, though the wife had so recently been in *articulo mortis*."

S. Hurok is probably America's number one music manager. For a fifth of a century he has been handling artists—such world-famous artists as Chaliapin, Isadora Duncan, and Pavlova. Mr. Hurok told me that one of the first lessons he learned in dealing with his temperamental stars was the necessity for sympathy, sympathy, and more sympathy with their ridiculous idiosyncrasies.

For three years, he was impresario for Feodor Chaliapin —one of the greatest bassos who ever thrilled the ritzy boxholders at the Metropolitan. Yet Chaliapin was a constant problem. He carried on like a spoiled child. To put it in Mr. Hurok's own inimitable phrase: "He was a hell of a fellow in every way."

For example, Chaliapin would call up Mr. Hurok about noon of the day he was going to sing and say, "Sol, I feel terrible. My throat is like raw hamburger. It is impossible

for me to sing tonight." Did Mr. Hurok argue with him?
Oh, no. He knew that an *entrepreneur* couldn't handle
artists that way. So he would rush over to Chaliapin's hotel,
dripping with sympathy. "What a pity," he would mourn.
"What a pity! My poor fellow. Of course, you cannot sing.
I will cancel the engagement at once. It will only cost you
a couple of thousand dollars, but that is nothing in comparison to your reputation."

Then Chaliapin would sigh and say, "Perhaps you had
better come over later in the day. Come at five and see how
I feel then."

At five o'clock, Mr. Hurok would again rush to his hotel,
dripping with sympathy. Again he would insist on can-
celing the engagement and again Chaliapin would sigh and
say, "Well, maybe you had better come to see me later. I
may be better then."

At 7:30 the great basso would consent to sing, only with
the understanding that Mr. Hurok would walk out on the
stage of the Metropolitan and announce that Chaliapin had
a very bad cold and was not in good voice. Mr. Hurok
would lie and say he would do it, for he knew that was the
only way to get the basso out on the stage.

Dr. Arthur I. Gates says in his splendid book, *Educational Psychology:* "Sympathy the human species universally craves. The child eagerly displays his injury; or even
inflicts a cut or bruise in order to reap abundant sympathy.
For the same purpose adults . . . show their bruises, relate
their accidents, illnesses, especially details of surgical operations. 'Self-pity' for misfortunes real or imaginary is, in
some measure, practically a universal practice."

So, if you want to win people to your way of thinking,
Rule 9 is:

*Be sympathetic with the other person's ideas and
desires.*

CHAPTER TEN

An Appeal That
Everybody Likes

I WAS REARED on the edge of the Jesse James country out in Missouri and I have visited the James farm at Kearney, Missouri, where the son of Jesse James is still living.

His wife told me stories of how Jesse robbed trains and held up banks and then gave money to the neighboring farmers to pay off their mortgages.

Jesse James probably regarded himself as an idealist at heart, just as Dutch Schultz, "Two Gun" Crowley, and Al Capone did two generations later. The fact is that every man you meet—even the man you see in the mirror—has a high regard for himself, and likes to be fine and unselfish in his own estimation.

J. Pierpont Morgan observed, in one of his analytical interludes, that a man usually has two reasons for doing a thing: one that sounds good and a real one.

The man himself will think of the real reason. You don't need to emphasize that. But all of us, being idealists at heart, like to think of the motives that sound good. So, in order to change people, appeal to the nobler motives.

Is that too idealistic to work in business? Let's see. Let's take the case of Hamilton J. Farrell of the Farrell-Mitchell Company of Glenolden, Pennsylvania. Mr. Farrell had a disgruntled tenant who threatened to move. The tenant's lease still had four months to run, at fifty-five dollars a month; nevertheless, he served notice that he was vacating immediately, regardless of lease.

"These people had lived in my house all winter—the most expensive part of the year," Mr. Farrell said as he told the story to the class, "and I knew it would be difficult to rent the apartment again before fall. I could see two hundred and twenty dollars going over the hill—and believe me, I saw red.

"Now, ordinarily, I would have waded into that tenant and advised him to read his lease again. I would have pointed out that if he moved, the full balance of his rent would fall due at once—and that I could, *and would*, move to collect.

"However, instead of flying off the handle and making a scene, I decided to try other tactics. So I started like this: 'Mr. Doe,' I said, 'I have listened to your story, and I still don't believe you intend to move. Years in the renting business have taught me something about human nature, and I sized you up in the first place as being a man of your word. In fact, I'm so sure of it that I'm willing to take the gamble.

" 'Now, here's my proposition. Lay your decision on the table for a few days and think it over. If you come back to me between now and the first of the month, when your rent is due, and tell me you still intend to move, I give you my word I will accept your decision as final. I will privilege you to move, and admit to myself I've been wrong in my judgment. But, I still believe you're a man of your word and will live up to your contract. For after all, we are either men or monkeys—and the choice usually lies with ourselves!'

"Well, when the new month came around, this gentleman came and paid his rent in person. He and his wife had talked it over, he said—and decided to stay. They had concluded that the only honorable thing to do was to live up to their lease."

When the late Nord Northcliffe found a newspaper using a picture of himself which he didn't want published, he wrote the editor a letter. But did he say, "Please do not publish that picture of me any more; *I* don't like it"? No, he appealed to a nobler motive. He appealed to the respect and love that all of us have for motherhood. He wrote, "Please do not publish that picture of me any more. My *mother* doesn't like it."

When John D. Rockefeller, Jr., wished to stop newspaper photographers from snapping pictures of his children, he, too, appealed to the nobler motives. He didn't say: *"I* don't want their pictures published." No, he appealed to the desire, deep in all of us, to refrain from harming children. He said: "You know how it is boys. You've got children yourselves, some of you. And you know it's not good for youngsters to get too much publicity."

When Cyrus H. K. Curtis, the poor boy from Maine, was starting on his meteoric career which was destined to make him millions as owner of *The Saturday Evening Post* and the *Ladies Home Journal*—when he first started, he couldn't afford to pay the prices that other magazines paid. He couldn't afford to hire first-class authors to write for money alone. So he appealed to their nobler motives. For example, he persuaded even Louisa May Alcott, the immortal author of *Little Women,* to write for him when she was at the flood tide of her fame; and he did it by offering to send a check for a hundred dollars, not to her, but to her favorite charity.

Right here the skeptic may say: "Oh, that stuff is all right for Northcliffe and Rockefeller or a sentimental novelist. But, boy! I'd like to see you make it work with the tough babies I have to collect bills from!"

You may be right. Nothing will work in all cases—and nothing will work with all men. If you are satisfied with the results you are now getting, why change? If you are not satisfied, why not experiment?

At any rate, I think you will enjoy reading this true story told by James L. Thomas, a former student of mine:

Six customers of a certain automobile company refused to pay their bills for servicing. No customer protested the entire bill but each one claimed that some one charge was wrong. In each case, the customer had signed for the work done, so the company knew it was right—and *said* so. That was the first mistake.

Here are the steps the men in the credit department took to collect these overdue bills. Do you suppose they succeeded?

1. They called on each customer and told him bluntly that they had come to collect a bill that was long past due.

2. They made it very plain that the company was absolutely and unconditionally right; therefore he, the customer, was absolutely and unconditionally wrong.

3. They intimated that they, the company, knew more about automobiles than he could ever hope to know. So what was the argument about?

4. Result: they argued.

Did any of these methods reconcile the customer and settle the account? You can answer that one yourself.

At this stage of affairs, the credit manager was about to open fire with a battery of legal talent, when fortunately the matter came to the attention of the general manager. The manager investigated these defaulting clients, and discovered that they all had the reputation of paying their bills promptly. Something was wrong here—something was drastically wrong about the method of collection. So he called in James L. Thomas and told him to collect these "uncollectible accounts."

These are the steps Mr. Thomas took.

1. "My visit to each customer," says Mr. Thomas, "was likewise to collect a bill long past due—a bill that we knew was absolutely right. But I didn't say a word

about that. I explained I had called to find out what it was the company had done, or failed to do."

2. "I made it clear that, until I had heard the customer's story, I had no opinion to offer. I told him the company made no claims to being infallible."

3. "I told him I was interested only in his car, and that he knew more about his car than anyone else in the world; that he was the authority on the subject."

4. "I let him talk, and I listened to him with all the interest and sympathy that he wanted—and had expected."

5. "Finally, when the customer was in a reasonable mood, I put the whole thing up to his sense of fair play. I appealed to the nobler motives. 'First,' I said, 'I want you to know that I also feel this matter has been badly mishandled. You have been inconvenienced and annoyed and irritated by one of our representatives. That should never have happened. I'm sorry and, as a representative of the company, I apologize. As I sat here and listened to your side of the story, I could not help being impressed by your fairness and patience. And now, because you are fairminded and patient, I am going to ask you to do something for me. It's something that you can do better than anyone else, something you know more about than anyone else. Here is this bill of yours; I know that it is safe for me to ask you to adjust it, just as you would do if you were the president of my company. I am going to leave it all up to you. Whatever you say goes.'

"Did he adjust the bill? He certainly did, and got quite a kick out of it. The bills ranged from $150 to $400—but did the customer give himself the best of it? Yes, one of them did! One of them refused to pay a penny of the disputed charge; but the other five all gave the company the best of it! And here's the cream of the whole thing—we delivered new cars to all six of these customers within the next two years!"

"Experience has taught me," says Mr. Thomas, "that when no information can be secured about the customer, the only sound basis on which to proceed is to assume that he is sincere, honest, truthful, and willing and anxious to pay the charges, once he is convinced they are correct. To put it differently and perhaps more clearly, people are honest and want to discharge their obligations. The exceptions to that rule are comparatively few, and I am convinced that the individual who is inclined to chisel will in most cases react favorably if you make him feel that you consider him honest, upright, and fair."

So, if you want to win people to your way of thinking, it is a fine thing, in general, to follow **Rule 10:**

Appeal to the nobler motives.

CHAPTER ELEVEN

The Movies Do It. Radio Does It. Why Don't You Do It?

A FEW YEARS AGO, the *Philadelphia Evening Bulletin* was being slandered by a dangerous whispering campaign. A malicious rumor was being circulated. Advertisers were being told that the newspaper carried too much advertising and too little news, that it was no longer attractive to readers. Immediate action was necessary. The gossip had to be squelched.

But how?

This is the way it was done.

The *Bulletin* clipped from its regular edition all reading matter of all kinds on one average day, classified it, and published it as a book. The book was called *One Day*. It contained 307 pages—as many as a two-dollar book; yet the *Bulletin* had printed all this news and feature material on one day and sold it, not for two dollars, but for two cents.

The printing of that book dramatized the fact that the *Bulletin* carried an enormous amount of interesting reading matter. It conveyed the facts more vividly, more interestingly, more impressively, than days of figures and mere talk could have done.

Read *Showmanship in Business* by Kenneth Goode and Zenn Kaufman—an exciting panorama of how showmen are ringing the cash register. It tells how Electrolux sells refrigerators by lighting matches at prospects' ears to dramatize the silence of their refrigerator. . . . How Personality enters Sears Roebuck catalogs with $1.95 hats autographed by Ann Sothern. . . . How George Wellbaum reveals that when a moving window display is stopped 80% of the audience is lost. . . . How Percy Whiting sells securities by showing prospects two lists of bonds—each list worth $1000 five years ago. He asks prospects which list they would buy. Presto! Current market figures reveal that one list (his, of course) appreciated. The element of *curiosity* holds the prospects' attention. . . . How Mickey Mouse nibbles his way into the Encyclopedia and how his name on toys pulls a factory out of bankruptcy. . . . How Eastern Air Lines packs them in on the sidewalk with a window reproducing the actual control panels of a Douglas Airliner. . . . How Harry Alexander excites his salesmen with a broadcast of an imaginary boxing bout between his product and a competitor's. . . . How a spot-light accidentally falls on a candy display—doubles sales. . . . How Chrysler stands elephants on his cars to prove toughness.

Richard Borden and Alvin Busse of New York University analyzed 15,000 sales interviews. They wrote a book entitled *How to Win an Argument,* then presented the same principles in a lecture, "Six Principles of Selling." This was subsequently made into a movie and shown before the sales forces of hundreds of large corporations. They not only explain the principles uncovered by their research—but they actually enact them. They wage verbal battles in front of an audience, showing wrong and right ways to make a sale.

This is the day of dramatization. Merely stating a truth isn't enough. The truth has to be made vivid, interesting, dramatic. You have to use showmanship. The movies do it.

Radio does it. And you will have to do it if you want attention.

Experts in window display know the trenchant power of dramatization. For example, the manufacturers of a new rat poison gave dealers a window display that included two live rats. The week the rats were shown, sales zoomed to five times their normal rate.

James B. Boynton of *The American Weekly* had to present a lengthy market report. His firm had just finished an exhaustive study for a leading brand of cold cream. Data was needed immediately on the menace of cut-rates; the prospect was one of the biggest—and most formidable—men in the advertising business.

And already his first approach had failed.

"The first time I went in," Mr. Boynton admits, "I found myself sidetracked into a futile discussion of the methods used in the investigation. He argued and I argued. He told me I was wrong, and I tried to prove that I was right.

"I finally won my point, to my own satisfaction—but my time was up, the interview was over, and I still hadn't produced results.

"The second time, I didn't bother with tabulations of figures and data. I went to see this man, I dramatized my facts.

"As I entered his office, he was busy at the phone. While he finished his conversation, I opened a suitcase and dumped thirty-two jars of cold cream on top of his desk —all products he knew—all competitors of his cream.

"On each jar, I had a tag itemizing the results of the trade investigation. And each tag told its story briefly, dramatically."

"What happened?"

"There was no longer any argument. Here was something new, something different. He picked up first one and then another of the cold-cream jars and read the information on the tag. A friendly conversation developed. He asked additional questions. He was intensely interested. He had originally given me only ten minutes to present my facts, but ten minutes passed, twenty minutes, forty minutes, and at the end of an hour we were still talking.

"I was presenting the same facts this time that I had presented previously. But this time I was using dramatization, showmanship—and what a difference it made."

Therefore, if you want to win people to your way of thinking, **Rule 11** is:

Dramatize your ideas.

CHAPTER TWELVE

When Nothing Else Works, Try This

CHARLES SCHWAB had a mill manager whose men weren't producing their quota of work.

"How is it," Schwab asked, "that a man as capable as you can't make this mill turn out what it should?"

"I don't know," the man replied, "I've coaxed the men; I've pushed them; I've sworn and cussed; I've threatened them with damnation and being fired. But nothing works. They just won't produce."

It happened to be the end of the day, just before the night shift came on.

"Give me a piece of chalk," Schwab said. Then, turning to the nearest man: "How many heats did your shift make today?"

"Six."

Without another word, Schwab chalked a big figure six on the floor, and walked away.

When the night shift came in, they saw the "6" and asked what it meant.

"The big boss was in here today," the day men said.

"He asked us how many heats we made, and we told him six. He chalked it down on the floor."

The next morning Schwab walked through the mill again. The night shift had rubbed out "6," and replaced it with a big "7."

When the day shift reported for work the next morning, they saw a big "7" chalked on the floor. So the night shift thought they were better than the day shift, did they? Well, they would show the night shift a thing or two. They pitched in with enthusiasm and when they quit that night, they left behind them an enormous, swaggering "10." Things were stepping up.

Shortly this mill, that had been lagging way behind in production, was turning out more work than any other mill in the plant.

The principle?

Let Charles Schwab say it in his own words. "The way to get things done," said Schwab, "is to stimulate competition. I do not mean in a sordid, money-getting way, but in the desire to excel."

The desire to excel! The challenge! Throwing down the gauntlet! An infallible way of appealing to men of spirit.

Without a challenge Theodore Roosevelt would never have been President of the United States. The Rough Rider, just back from Cuba, was picked for Governor of New York State. The opposition discovered he was no longer a legal resident of that state; and Roosevelt, frightened, wished to withdraw. Then Thomas Collier Platt threw down the gage. Turning suddenly on Theodore Roosevelt, he cried in a ringing voice: "Is the hero of San Juan Hill a coward?"

Roosevelt stayed in the fight—and the rest is history. A challenge not only changed his life; it had a real effect upon the history of this nation.

Charles Schwab knew the enormous power of a challenge. So did Boss Platt and so did Al Smith.

When Al Smith was Governor of New York, he was up

against it. Sing Sing, the most notorious penitentiary west of Devil's Island, was without a warden. Scandals had been sweeping through the prison walls, scandals and ugly rumors. Smith needed a strong man to rule Sing Sing— an iron man. But who? He sent for Lewis E. Lawes of New Hampton.

"How about going up to take charge of Sing Sing?" he said jovially, when Lawes stood before him. "They need a man up there with experience."

Lawes was stumped. He knew the dangers of Sing Sing. It was a political appointment, subject to the vagaries of political whims. Wardens had come and gone—one had lasted only three weeks. He had a career to consider. Was it worth the risk?

And then Smith, who saw his hesitation, leaned back and smiled. "Young fellow," he said, "I don't blame you for being scared. It's a tough spot. It'll take a big man to go up there and stay."

So Smith was throwing down a challenge, was he? Lawes liked the idea of attempting a job that called for a big man.

So he went. And he stayed. He stayed, to become the most famous warden alive. His book, *20,000 Years in Sing Sing,* sold into the hundreds of thousands of copies. He has broadcast on the air; his stories of prison life have inspired dozens of movies. And his "humanizing" of criminals has wrought miracles in the way of prison reform.

"I have never found," said Harvey S. Firestone, founder of the great Firestone Tire & Rubber Company, "that pay and pay alone would either bring together or hold good men. I think it was the game itself . . ."

That is what every successful man loves: the game. The chance for self-expression. The chance to prove his worth, to excel, to win. That is what makes foot races and hog-calling and pie-eating contests. The desire to excel. The desire for a feeling of importance.

So, if you want to win men—spirited men, men of mettle—to your way of thinking, **Rule 12** is this:

Throw down a challenge.

Twelve Ways of Winning People to Your Way of Thinking

RULE 1: The only way to get the best of an argument is to avoid it.

RULE 2: Show respect for the other man's opinions. Never tell a man he is wrong.

RULE 3: If you are wrong, admit it quickly and emphatically.

RULE 4: Begin in a friendly way.

RULE 5: Get the other person saying "yes, yes" immediately.

RULE 6: Let the other man do a great deal of the talking.

RULE 7: Let the other man feel that the idea is his.

RULE 8: Try honestly to see things from the other person's point of view.

RULE 9: Be sympathetic with the other person's ideas and desires.

RULE 10: Appeal to the nobler motives.

RULE 11: Dramatize your ideas.

RULE 12: Throw down a challenge.

PART FOUR

Nine Ways to Change People Without Giving Offense Or Arousing Resentment

CHAPTER ONE

If You Must Find Fault, This is the Way to Begin

A FRIEND OF MINE was a guest at the White House for a weekend during the administration of Calvin Coolidge. Drifting into the President's private office, he heard Coolidge say to one of his secretaries, "That's a pretty dress you are wearing this morning, and you are a very attractive young woman."

That was probably the most effulgent praise Silent Cal had ever bestowed upon a secretary in his life. It was so unusual, so unexpected, that the girl blushed in confusion. Then Coolidge said, "Now, don't get stuck up. I just said that to make you feel good. From now on, I wish you would be a little bit more careful with your punctuation."

His method was probably a bit obvious, but the psychology was superb. It is always easier to listen to un-

186

pleasant things after we have heard some praise of our good points.

A barber lathers a man before he shaves him; and that is precisely what McKinley did back in 1896, when he was running for President. One of the prominent Republicans of that day had written a campaign speech that he felt was just a trifle better than Cicero and Patrick Henry and Daniel Webster all rolled into one. With great glee, this chap read his immortal speech aloud to McKinley. The speech had its fine points, but it just wouldn't do. It would have raised a tornado of criticism. McKinley didn't want to hurt the man's feelings. He must not kill the man's splendid enthusiasm, and yet he had to say "no." Note how adroitly he did it.

"My friend, that is a splendid speech, a magnificent speech," McKinley said. "No one could have prepared a better one. There are many occasions on which it would be precisely the right thing to say; but is it quite suitable to this peculiar occasion? Sound and sober as it is from your standpoint, I must consider its effect from the party's standpoint. Now you go home and write a speech along the lines I indicate, and send me a copy of it."

He did just that. McKinley blue-penciled and helped him rewrite his second speech; and he became one of the effective speakers of the campaign.

Here is the second most famous letter that Abraham Lincoln ever wrote. (His most famous one was written to Mrs. Bixby, expressing his sorrow for the death of the five sons she had lost in battle.) Lincoln probably dashed this letter off in five minutes; yet it sold at public auction in 1926 for twelve thousand dollars. And that, by the way, is more money than Lincoln was able to save by half a century of hard work.

This letter was written on April 26, 1863, during the darkest period of the Civil War. For eighteen months, Lincoln's generals had been leading the Union Army from one tragic defeat to another. Nothing but futile, stupid, human butchery. The nation was appalled. Thousands of soldiers deserted from the army; and even the Republican members of the Senate revolted and wanted to force Lincoln out of the White House. "We are now on the brink of destruction," Lincoln said. "It appears to me that even the Almighty is against us. I can hardly see a ray of hope." Such was the period of black sorrow and chaos out of which this letter came.

I am printing the letter here because it shows how Lincoln tried to change an obstreperous general when the very fate of the nation might depend upon the general's actions.

This is perhaps the sharpest letter Abe Lincoln wrote after he became President; yet you will note that he praised General Hooker before he spoke of his grave faults.

Yes, they were grave faults; but Lincoln didn't call them that. Lincoln was more conservative, more diplomatic. Lincoln wrote: "There are some things in regard to which I am not quite satisfied with you." Talk about tact! And diplomacy!

Here is the letter addressed to Major General Hooker:

I have placed you at the head of the Army of the Potomac. Of course, I have done this upon what appear to me to be sufficient reasons, and yet I think it best for you to know that there are some things in regard to which I am not quite satisfied with you.

I believe you to be a brave and skillful soldier, which, of course, I like. I also believe you do not mix politics with your profession, in which you are right. You have confidence in yourself, which is a valuable if not an indispensable quality.

You are ambitious, which, within reasonable bounds, does good rather than harm. But I think that during General Burnside's command of the army you have taken counsel of your ambition and thwarted him as much as you could, in which you did a great wrong to the country and to a most meritorious and honorable brother officer.

I have heard, in such a way as to believe it, of your recently saying that both the army and the Government needed a dictator. Of course, it was not for this, but in spite of it, that I have given you command.

Only those generals who gain successes can set up as dictators. What I now ask of you is military success and I will risk the dictatorship.

The Government will support you to the utmost of its ability, which is neither more nor less than it has done and will do for all commanders. I much fear that the spirit which you have aided to infuse into the army, of criticizing their commander and withholding confidence from him, will now turn upon you. I shall assist you, as far as I can, to put it down.

Neither you nor Napoleon, if he were alive again, could get any good out of an army while such spirit prevails in it, and now beware of rashness. Beware of rashness, but with energy and sleepless vigilance go forward and give us victories.

You are not a Coolidge, a McKinley, or a Lincoln. You want to know whether this philosophy will operate for you in everyday business contacts. Will it? Let's see. Let's take the case of W. P. Gaw of the Wark Company, Philadelphia. Mr. Gaw is an ordinary citizen like you and me. He was a member of one of the courses I conducted in Philadelphia, and he related this incident in one of the speeches given before the class.

The Wark Company had contracted to build and complete a large office building in Philadelphia by a certain specified date. Everything was going along according to Hoyle, the building was almost finished, when suddenly the subcontractor making the ornamental bronze work to go on the exterior of the building declared that he couldn't make delivery on schedule. What! An entire building held up! Heavy penalties! Distressing losses! All because of one man!

Long-distance telephone calls. Arguments! Heated conversations! All in vain Then Mr Gaw was sent to New York to beard the bronze lion in his den.

"Do you know you are the only man in Brooklyn with your name?" Mr. Gaw asked as he entered the president's office. The president was surprised. "No, I didn't know that."

"Well," said Mr. Gaw, "when I got off the train this morning, I looked in the telephone book to get your address, and you are the only man in the Brooklyn phone book with your name."

"I never knew that," the president said. He examined the phone book with interest. "Well, it's an unusual name," he said proudly. "My family came from Holland and settled in New York almost two hundred years ago." He continued to talk about his family and his ancestors for several minutes. When he finished that, Mr. Gaw complimented him on how large a plant he had, and compared it favorably with a number of similar plants he had visited. "It is one of the cleanest and neatest bronze factories I ever saw," said Gaw.

"I have spent a lifetime building up this business," the president said, "and I am rather proud of it. Would you like to take a look around the factory?"

During this tour of inspection, Mr. Gaw complimented him on his system of fabrication, and told him how and why it seemed superior to those of some of his competitors. Mr. Gaw commented on some unusual machines, and the president announced that he himself had invented those machines. He spent considerable time showing Mr. Gaw how they operated, and the superior work they turned out. He insisted on taking Mr. Gaw to lunch. So far, mind you, not a word had been said about the real purpose of Mr. Gaw's visit.

After lunch, the president said, "Now, to get down to business. Naturally, I know why you are here. I did not expect that our meeting would be so enjoyable. You can go back to Philadelphia with my promise that your material will be fabricated and shipped, even if other orders have to be delayed."

Mr. Gaw got everything that he wanted without even asking for it. The material arrived on time, and the building was completed the day the completion contract expired.

Would this have happened had Mr. Gaw used the hammer and dynamite method generally employed on such occasions?

To change people without giving offense or arousing resentment, **Rule 1** is:

Begin with praise and honest appreciation.

CHAPTER TWO

How to Criticize—and Not Be Hated for It

CHARLES SCHWAB was passing through one of his steel mills one day at noon when he came across some of his employees smoking. Immediately above their heads was a sign which said "No Smoking." Did Schwab point to the sign and say, "Can't you read?" Oh, no, not Schwab. He walked over to the men, handed each one a cigar, and said, "I'll appreciate it, boys, if you will smoke these on the outside." They knew that he knew that they had broken a rule—and they admired him because he said nothing about it and gave them a little present and made them feel important. Couldn't keep from loving a man like that, could you?

John Wanamaker used the same technique. Wanamaker used to make a tour of his great store in Philadelphia every day. Once he saw a customer waiting at a counter. No one was paying the slightest attention to her. The sales people? Oh, they were in a huddle at the far end of the counter laughing and talking among themselves. Wanamaker didn't say a word. Quietly slipping behind the counter, he waited on the woman himself and then handed the purchase to the sales people to be wrapped as he went on his way.

On March 8, 1887, the eloquent Henry Ward Beecher died, or changed worlds, as the Japanese say. The following Sunday, Lyman Abbott was invited to speak in the pulpit left silent by Beecher's passing. Eager to do his best, he wrote, rewrote, and polished his sermon with the meticulous care of a Flaubert. Then he read it to his wife. It was poor—as most written speeches are. She might have said, if she had had less judgment, "Lyman, that is terrible. That'll never do. You'll put people to sleep. It reads like an encyclopedia. You ought to know better than that after all the years you have been preaching. For heaven's sake, why don't you talk like a human being? Why don't you act natural? You'll disgrace yourself if you ever read that stuff."

That's what she *might* have said. And, if she had, you know what would have happened. And she knew too. So, she merely remarked that it would make an excellent article for the *North American Review*. In other words, she praised it and at the same time subtly suggested that it wouldn't do as a speech. Lyman Abbott saw the point, tore up his carefully prepared manuscript, and preached without even using notes.

To change people without giving offense or arousing resentment, **Rule 2** is:

Call attention to people's mistakes indirectly.

CHAPTER THREE

Talk About Your Own Mistakes First

A FEW YEARS AGO, my niece, Josephine Carnegie, left her home in Kansas City and came to New York to act as my secretary. She was nineteen, had graduated from high school three years previously, and her business experience was a trifle more than zero. Today she is one of the most perfect secretaries west of Suez; but, in the beginning, she was—well, susceptible to improvement. One day when I started to criticize her, I said to myself: "Just a minute, Dale Carnegie; just a minute. You are twice as old as Josephine. You have had ten thousand times as much business experience. How can you possibly expect her to have your viewpoint, your judgment, your initiative— mediocre though they may be? And just a minute, Dale, what were you doing at nineteen? Remember the asinine mistakes, the fool blunders you made? Remember the time you did this . . . and that . . .?"

After thinking the matter over, honestly and impartially, I concluded that Josephine's batting average at nineteen was better than mine had been—and that, I'm sorry to confess, isn't paying Josephine much of a compliment.

So after that, when I wanted to call Josephine's attention to a mistake, I used to begin by saying, "You have made a mistake, Josephine, but the Lord knows, it's no worse than many I have made. You were not born with judgment. That comes only with experience; and you are better than I was at your age. I have been guilty of so many stupid, silly things myself I have very little inclination to criticize you or anyone. But don't you think it would have been wiser if you had done so and so?"

It isn't nearly so difficult to listen to a recital of your own faults if the criticizer begins by humbly admitting that he, too, is far from impeccable.

The polished Prince von Bulow learned the sharp necessity of doing this back in 1909. Von Bulow was then the Imperial Chancellor of Germany, and on the throne sat Wilhelm II—Wilhelm, the haughty; Wilhelm, the arrogant; Wilhelm, the last of the German Kaisers, building an army and navy which he boasted could whip their weight in wild cats.

Then an astonishing thing happened. The Kaiser said things, incredible things, things that rocked the continent and started a series of explosions heard around the world. To make matters infinitely worse, the Kaiser made these silly, egotistical, absurd announcements in public, he made them while he was a guest in England, and he gave his royal permission to have them printed in the *Daily Telegraph*. For example, he declared that he was the only German who felt friendly toward the English; that he was constructing a navy against the menace of Japan; that he, and he alone, had saved England from being humbled in the dust by Russia and France; that it was *his* plan of campaign that enabled England's Lord Roberts to defeat the Boers in South Africa; and so on and on.

No other such amazing words had ever fallen from the lips of a European king in peace time within a hundred years. The entire continent buzzed with the fury of a hornets' nest. England was incensed. German statesmen were aghast. And in the midst of all this consternation, the Kaiser became panicky, and suggested to Prince von Bulow, the Imperial Chancellor, that he take the blame. Yes, he wanted von Bulow to announce that it was all his responsibility, that he had advised his monarch to say these incredible things.

"But Your Majesty," von Bulow protested, "it seems to me utterly impossible that anybody either in Germany or England could suppose me capable of having advised Your Majesty to say any such thing."

The moment those words were out of von Bulow's mouth, he realized he had made a grave mistake. The Kaiser blew up.

"You consider me a donkey," he shouted, "capable of blunders you yourself could never have committed!"

Von Bulow knew that he ought to have praised before he condemned; but since that was too late, he did the next best thing. He praised after he had criticized. And it worked a miracle—as praise often does.

"I'm far from suggesting that," he answered respectfully. "Your Majesty surpasses me in many respects; not only, of course, in naval and military knowledge, but, above all, in natural science. I have often listened in admiration when Your Majesty explained the barometer, or wireless telegraphy, or the Röntgen rays. I am shamefully ignorant of all branches of natural science, have no notion of chemistry or physics, and am quite incapable of explaining the simplest of natural phenomena. But," von Bulow continued, "in compensation, I possess some historical knowledge and perhaps certain qualities useful in politics, especially in diplomacy."

The Kaiser beamed. Von Bulow had praised him. Von Bulow had exalted him and humbled himself. The Kaiser could forgive anything after that. "Haven't I always told you," he exclaimed with enthusiasm, "that we complement one another famously? We should stick together, and we will!"

He shook hands with von Bulow, not once, but several times. And later in the day he waxed so enthusiastic that he exclaimed with doubled fists, "If anyone says anything to me against Prince von Bulow, *I shall punch him in the nose!*"

Von Bulow saved himself in time—but, canny diplomat that he was, he nevertheless had made one error: he should have *begun* by talking about his own shortcomings and Wilhelm's superiority—not by intimating that the Kaiser was a half-wit in need of a guardian.

If a few sentences humbling oneself and praising the other party can turn a haughty, insulated Kaiser into a staunch friend, imagine what humility and praise can do for you and me in our daily contacts. Rightfully used, they will work veritable miracles in human relations.

To change people without giving offense or arousing resentment, **Rule 3** is:

Talk about your own mistakes before criticizing the other person.

CHAPTER FOUR

No One Likes to Take Orders

I RECENTLY had the pleasure of dining with Miss Ida Tarbell, the dean of American biographers. When I told her I was writing this book, we began discussing this all-important subject of getting along with people, and she told me that while she was writing her biography of Owen D. Young she interviewed a man who had sat for three years in the same office with Mr. Young. This man declared that during all that time he had never heard Owen D. Young give a direct order to anyone. He always gave suggestions, not orders. Owen D. Young never said, for example, "Do this or do that," or "Don't do this or don't do that." He would say, "You might consider this," or "Do you think that would work?" Frequently he would say, after he had dictated a letter, "What do you think of this?" In looking over a letter of one of his assistants, he would say, "Maybe if we were to phrase it this way it would be better." He always gave a person an opportunity to do things himself; he never told his assistants to do things; he let them do them, let them learn from their mistakes.

A technique like that makes it easy for a person to correct his error. A technique like that saves a man's pride and gives him a feeling of importance. It makes him want to co-operate instead of rebel.

To change people without giving offense or arousing resentment, **Rule 4** is:

Ask questions instead of giving direct orders.

CHAPTER FIVE

Let the Other Man Save His Face

YEARS AGO the General Electric Company was faced with the delicate task of removing Charles Steinmetz from the head of a department. Steinmetz, a genius of the first magnitude when it came to electricity, was a washout as the head of the calculating department. Yet the company didn't dare offend the man. He was indispensable—and highly sensitive. So they gave him a new title. They made him Consulting Engineer of the General Electric Company —a new title for work he was already doing—and let someone else head up the department.

Steinmetz was happy.

So were the officers of the G.E. They had gently maneuvered their most temperamental star, and they had done it without a storm—by letting him save face.

Letting him save his face! How important, how vitally important that is! And how few of us ever stop to think of it! We ride roughshod over the feelings of others, getting our own way, finding fault, issuing threats, criticizing a child or an employee in front of others, without even considering the hurt to the other person's pride! Whereas a few minutes' thought, a considerate word or two, a genuine understanding of the other person's attitude would go so far toward alleviating the sting!

Let's remember that the next time we are faced with the distasteful necessity of discharging a servant or an employee.

"Firing employees is not much fun. Getting fired is even less fun." (I'm quoting now from a letter written me by Marshall A. Granger, certified public accountant.) "Our business is mostly seasonal. Therefore we have to let a lot of men go in March.

"It's a byword in our profession that no one enjoys wielding the ax. Consequently, the custom has developed of getting it over as soon as possible, and usually in the following way: 'Sit down, Mr. Smith. The season's over, and we don't seem to see any more assignments for you. Of course, you understood that you were employed only for the busy season anyhow, etc., etc.'

"The effect on the men was one of disappointment, and a feeling of being 'let down.' Most of them were in the accounting field for life, and they retained no particular love for the firm that dropped them so casually.

"I recently decided to let our extra men go with a little more tact and consideration. So I have called each man in only after carefully thinking over his work during the winter. And I've said something like this: 'Mr. Smith, you've done a fine job (if he has). That time we sent you over to Newark, you had a tough assignment. You were on the spot, but you came through with flying colors, and we want you to know the firm is proud of you. You've got the stuff—you're going a long way, wherever you're working. This firm believes in you, and is rooting for you, and we don't want you to forget it!'

"Effect? The men go away feeling a lot better about being fired. They don't feel 'let down.' They know if we had work for them, we'd keep them on. And when we need them again, they come to us with a keen personal affection."

The late Dwight Morrow possessed an uncanny ability to reconcile belligerents who wanted to fly at each other's throats. How? He scrupulously sought what was right and just on both sides—he praised it, emphasized it, brought it carefully to the light—and no matter what the settlement, he never placed any man in the wrong.

That's what every arbitrator knows—let men save their faces.

Really big men, the world over, are too big to waste time gloating over their personal triumphs. To illustrate:

In 1922, after centuries of bitter antagonism, the Turks determined to drive the Greeks forever from Turkish territory.

Mustapha Kemal made a Napoleonic speech to his soldiers, saying, "Your goal is the Mediterranean," and one of the bitterest wars in modern history was on. The Turks won; and when the two Greek generals, Tricoupis and Dionis, made their way to Kemal's headquarters to surrender, the Turkish people called down the curses of heaven upon their vanquished foes.

But Kemal's attitude was free from triumph.

"Sit down, gentlemen," he said, grasping their hands. "You must be tired." Then, after discussing the campaign in detail, he softened the blow of their defeat. "War," he said, as one soldier to another, "is a game in which the best men are sometimes worsted."

Even in the full flush of victory, Kemal remembered this important rule (**Rule 5** for us):

Let the other man save his face.

CHAPTER SIX

How to Spur Men on to Success

I USED TO KNOW Pete Barlow. Pete had a dog-and-pony act and he spent his life traveling with circuses and vaudeville shows. I loved to watch Pete train new dogs for his act. I noticed that the moment a dog showed the slightest improvement, Pete patted and praised him and gave him meat and made a great to-do about it.

That's nothing new. Animal trainers have been using that same technique for centuries.

Why, I wonder, don't we use the same common sense when trying to change people that we use when trying to change dogs? Why don't we use meat instead of a whip? Why don't we use praise instead of condemnation? Let's praise even the slightest improvement. That inspires the other fellow to keep on improving.

Warden Lewis E. Lawes has found that praising the slightest improvement pays, even with crime-hardened men in Sing Sing. "I have found," Warden Lawes said in a letter which I received while writing this chapter, "that the voicing of proper appreciation for the efforts of the inmates secures greater results in obtaining their co-operation and furthering their ultimate rehabilitation than harsh criticism and condemnation for their delinquencies."

I have never been incarcerated in Sing Sing—at least not yet—but I can look back in my own life and see where a few words of praise have sharply changed my entire future. Can't you say the same thing about your life? History is replete with striking ilustrations of the sheer witchery of praise.

For example, half a century ago, a boy of ten was working in a factory in Naples. He longed to be a singer, but his first teacher discouraged him. "You can't sing," he said. "You haven't any voice at all. It sounds like the wind in the shutters."

But his mother, a poor peasant woman, put her arms about him and praised him and told him she knew he could sing, she could already see an improvement, and she went barefoot in order to save money to pay for his music lessons. That peasant mother's praise and encouragement changed that boy's life. You may have heard of him. His name was Caruso.

Years ago, a young man in London aspired to be a writer. But everything seemed to be against him. He had never been able to attend school more than four years. His father had been flung in jail because he couldn't pay his debts, and this young man often knew the pangs of hunger. Finally, he got a job pasting labels on bottles of blacking in a rat-infested warehouse; and he slept at night in a dismal attic room with two other boys—gutter snipes from the slums of London. He had so little confidence in his ability to write that he sneaked out and mailed his first manuscript in the dead of night so nobody would laugh at him. Story after story was refused. Finally the great day came when one was accepted. True, he wasn't paid a shilling for it, but one editor had praised him. One editor had given him recognition. He was so thrilled that he wandered aimlessly around the streets with tears rolling down his cheeks.

The praise, the recognition that he received by getting one story in print, changed his whole career, for if it hadn't been for that encouragement, he might have spent his entire life working in rat-infested factories. You may have heard of that boy, too. His name was Charles Dickens.

Half a century ago, another boy in London was working as a clerk in a dry-goods store. He had to get up at five o'clock, sweep out the store, and slave for fourteen hours a day. It was sheer drudgery and he despised it. After two years, he could stand it no longer, so he got up one morning, and, without waiting for breakfast, tramped fifteen miles to talk to his mother, who was working as a housekeeper.

He was frantic. He pleaded with her. He wept. He swore he would kill himself if he had to remain in the shop any longer. Then he wrote a long, pathetic letter to his old schoolmaster, declaring that he was heartbroken, that he no longer wanted to live. His old schoolmaster gave him a little praise and assured him that he really was very intelligent and fitted for finer things and offered him a job as a teacher.

That praise changed the future of that boy and made a lasting impression on the history of English literature. For that boy has since written seventy-seven books and made over a million dollars with his pen. You've probably heard of him. His name is H. G. Wells.

Back in 1922, a young man was living out in California having a hard time trying to support his wife. He sang in a church choir on Sundays and picked up five dollars now and then by singing "Oh Promise Me" at a wedding. He was so hard up he couldn't live in town, so he rented a rickety house that stood in the middle of a vineyard. It cost him only $12.50 a month; but, low as this rent was, he couldn't pay it, and he got ten months behind. He worked in the vineyard picking grapes to pay off his rent. He told me there were times when he had very little else to eat but grapes. He was so discouraged that he was about ready to forego a career as a singer to sell automobile trucks for a living when Rupert Hughes praised him. Rupert Hughes said to him, "You have the makings of a great voice. You ought to study in New York."

That young man recently told me that little bit of praise, that slight encouragement, proved to be the turning point in his career, for it inspired him to borrow $2,500 and start East. You may have heard of him too. His name is Lawrence Tibbett.

Talk about changing people. If you and I will inspire the people with whom we come in contact to a realization of the hidden treasures they possess, we can do far more than change people. We can literally transform them.

Exaggeration? Then listen to these sage words from the late Professor William James of Harvard, perhaps the most distinguished psychologist and philosopher America ever produced:

> Compared with what we ought to be, we are only half awake. We are making use of only a small part of our physical and mental resources. Stating the thing broadly, the human individual thus lives far within his limits. He possesses powers of various sorts which he habitually fails to use.

Yes, you who are reading these lines possess powers of various sorts which you habitually fail to use; and one of these powers which you are probably not using to the fullest extent is your magic ability to praise people and inspire them with a realization of their latent possibilities.

So, to change people without giving offense or arousing resentment, **Rule 6** is:

Praise the slightest improvement and praise every improvement. Be "hearty in your approbation and lavish in your praise."

Give the Dog a Good Name

A FRIEND OF MINE, Mrs. Ernest Gent, 175 Brewster Road, Scarsdale, New York, hired a servant girl, telling her to report for work the following Monday. In the meantime, Mrs. Gent telephoned a woman who had formerly employed this girl. All was not well. When the girl came to start work, Mrs. Gent said: "Nellie, I telephoned the other day to a woman you used to work for. She said you were honest and reliable, a good cook and good at caring for the children. But she also said you were sloppy and never kept the house clean. Now I think she was lying. You dress neatly. Anybody can see that. And I'll bet you keep the house just as neat and clean as your person. You and I are going to get along fine."

And they did. Nellie had a reputation to live up to; and believe me, she did live up to it. She kept the house shining. She would gladly have scrubbed and dusted an extra hour a day rather than be untrue to Mrs. Gent's ideal of her.

"The average man," said Samuel Vauclain, president of

the Baldwin Locomotive Works, "can be led readily if you have his respect and if you show him that you respect him for some kind of ability."

In short, if you want to improve a person in a certain respect, act as though that particular trait were already one of his outstanding characteristics. Shakespeare said: "Assume a virtue if you have it not." And it might be well to assume and state openly that the other party has the virtue you want him to develop. Give him a fine reputation to live up to, and he will make prodigious efforts rather than see you disillusioned.

Georgette Leblanc, in her book, *Souvenirs, My Life with Maeterlinck,* describes the startling transformation of a humble Belgian Cinderella.

"A servant girl from a neighboring hotel brought my meals," she writes. "She was called 'Marie the Dishwasher' because she had started her career as a scullery assistant. She was a kind of monster, cross-eyed, bandy-legged, poor in flesh and spirit.

"One day, while she was holding my plate of macaroni in her red hands, I said to her point-blank, 'Marie, you do not know what treasures are within you.'

"Accustomed to holding back her emotions, Marie waited a few moments, not daring to risk the slightest gesture for fear of a catastrophe. Then she put the dish on the table, sighed, and said ingenuously, 'Madame, I would never have believed it.' She did not doubt, she did not ask a question. She simply went back to the kitchen and repeated what I had said, and such is the force of faith that no one made fun of her. From that day on, she was even given a certain consideration. But the most curious change of all occurred in the humble Marie herself. Believing she was the tabernacle of unseen marvels, she began taking care of her face and body so carefully that her starved youth seemed to bloom and modestly hide her plainness.

"Two months later, as I was leaving, she announced her coming marriage with the nephew of the chef. 'I'm going to be a lady,' she said and thanked me. A small phrase had changed her entire life."

Georgette Leblanc had given "Marie the Dishwasher" a

reputation to live up to—and that reputation transformed her.

Henry Clay Risner used the same technique when he wanted to influence the conduct of American doughboys in France. General James G. Harbord, one of the most popular American generals, had told Risner that in his opinion the two million doughboys in France were the cleanest and most idealistic men of whom he had ever read, or with whom he had ever come in contact.

Extravagant praise? Perhaps. But see how Risner used it.

"I never failed to tell the soldiers what the General had said," Risner writes. "Not for a moment did I question whether it was true or not, but I knew that, even were they not, the knowledge of General Harbord's opinion would inspire them to strive toward that standard."

There is an old saying: "Give a dog a bad name and you may as well hang him." But give him a good name—and see what happens!

Almost everyone—rich man, poor man, beggar man, thief—lives up to the reputation of honesty that is bestowed upon him.

"If you must deal with a crook," says Warden Lawes of Sing Sing—and the Warden ought to know what he's talking about—"If you must deal with a crook, there is only one possible way of getting the better of him—treat him as if he were an honorable gentleman. Take it for granted he is on the level. He will be so flattered by such treatment that he may answer to it, and be proud that someone trusts him."

That is so fine, so significant that I am going to repeat it: "If you must deal with a crook, there is only one possible way of getting the better of him—treat him as if he were an honorable gentleman. Take it for granted he is on the level. He will be so flattered by such treatment that he may answer to it, and be proud that someone trusts him."

So, if you want to influence the conduct of a man without arousing resentment or giving offense, remember **Rule 7:**

Give a man a fine reputation to live up to.

CHAPTER SEVEN

Make the Fault Seem Easy to Correct

A SHORT TIME AGO a bachelor friend of mine, about forty years old, became engaged, and his fiancée persuaded him to take some belated dancing lessons. "The Lord knows I needed dancing lessons," he confessed as he told me the story, "for I danced just as I did when I first started twenty years ago. The first teacher I engaged probably told me the truth. She said I was all wrong; I would just have to forget everything and begin all over again. But that took the heart out of me. I had no incentive to go on. So I quit her.

"The next teacher may have been lying; but I liked it. She said nonchalantly that my dancing was a bit old-fashioned perhaps, but the fundamentals were all right, and she assured me I wouldn't have any trouble learning a few new steps. The first teacher had discouraged me by emphasizing my mistakes. This new teacher did the opposite. She kept praising the things I did right and minimizing my errors. 'You have a natural sense of rhythm,' she assured me. 'You really are a natural born dancer.' Now my common sense tells me that I always have been and always will be a fourth-rate dancer; yet, deep in my heart, I still like to think that *maybe* she meant it. To be sure, I was paying her to say it; but why bring that up?

"At any rate, I know I am a better dancer than I would have been if she hadn't told me I had a natural sense of rhythm. That encouraged me. That gave me hope. That made me want to improve."

Tell a child, a husband, or an employee that he is stupid or dumb at a certain thing, that he has no gift for it, and that he is doing it all wrong and you have destroyed almost every incentive to try to improve. But use the opposite technique; be liberal with your encouragement; make the thing seem easy to do; let the other person know that you have faith in his ability to do it, that he has an undeveloped flair for it—and he will practice until the dawn comes in at the window in order to excel.

That is the technique that Lowell Thomas uses; and believe me, he is a superb artist in human relations. He builds you up. He gives you confidence. He inspires you with courage and faith. For example, I recently spent the week-end with Mr. and Mrs. Thomas; and, on Saturday night, I was asked to sit in on a friendly bridge game before a roaring fire. Bridge? I? Oh, no! No! No! Not me. I knew nothing about it. The game had always been a black mystery to me. No! No! Impossible!

"Why, Dale, it is no trick at all," Lowell replied. "There is nothing to bridge except memory and judgment. You once wrote a chapter on memory. Bridge will be a cinch for you. It is right up your alley."

And presto, almost before I realized what I was doing, I found myself for the first time at a bridge table. All because I was told I had a natural flair for it and the game was made to seem easy.

Speaking of bridge reminds me of Ely Culbertson. Culbertson's name is a household word wherever bridge is played; and his books on bridge have been translated into a dozen languages and a million copies have been sold. Yet he told me he never would have made a profession out of the game if a young woman hadn't assured him he had a flair for it.

When he came to America in 1922, he tried to get a job teaching philosophy and sociology, but he couldn't.

Then he tried selling coal, and he failed at that.

Then he tried selling coffee, and he failed at that, too.

It never occurred to him in those days to teach bridge. He was not only a poor card player, but he was also very stubborn. He asked so many questions and held so many post mortem examinations that no one wanted to play with him.

Then he met a pretty bridge teacher, Josephine Dillon, fell in love and married her. She noticed how carefully he analyzed his cards and persuaded him that he was a potential genius at the card table. It was that encouragement and that alone, Culbertson told me, that caused him to make a profession of bridge.

So, if you want to change people without giving offense or arousing resentment, **Rule 8** is:

Use encouragement. Make the fault you want to correct seem easy to correct; make the thing you want the other person to do seem easy to do.

CHAPTER NINE

Making People Glad
to Do What You Want

BACK IN 1915, America was aghast. For more than a year, the nations of Europe had been slaughtering one another on a scale never before dreamed of in all the bloody annals of mankind. Could peace be brought about? No one knew. But Woodrow Wilson was determined to try. He would send a personal representative, a peace emissary, to counsel with the war lords of Europe.

William Jennings Bryan, Secretary of State, Bryan, the peace advocate, longed to go. He saw a chance to perform a great service and make his name immortal. But Wilson appointed another man, his intimate friend, Colonel House; and it was House's thorny task to break the unwelcome news to Bryan without giving him offense.

"Bryan was distinctly disappointed when he heard I was to go to Europe as the peace emissary," Colonel House records in his diary. "He said he had planned to do this himself . . .

"I replied that the President thought it would be unwise

for anyone to do this officially, and *that his going would attract a great deal of attention* and people would wonder why he was there . . ."

You see the intimation? House practically tells Bryan that he is *too important* for the job—and Bryan is satisfied.

Colonel House, adroit, experienced in the ways of the world, was following one of the important rules of human relations: *Always make the other man happy about doing the thing you suggest.*

Woodrow Wilson followed that policy even when inviting William Gibbs McAdoo to become a member of his cabinet. That was the highest honor he could confer upon anyone, and yet Wilson did it in such way as to make the other man feel doubly important. Here is the story in McAdoo's own words: "He [Wilson] said that he was making up his cabinet and that he would be very glad if I would accept a place in it as Secretary of the Treasury. He had a delightful way of putting things; he created the impression that by accepting this great honor I would be doing him a favor."

Unfortunately, Wilson didn't always employ such tact. If he had, history might have been different. For example, Wilson didn't make the Senate and the Republican Party happy about putting the United States in the League of Nations. Wilson refused to take Elihu Root or Hughes or Henry Cabot Lodge or any other prominent Republican to the peace conference with him. Instead, he took along unknown men from his own party. He snubbed the Republicans, refused to let them feel that the League was their idea as well as his, refused to let them have a finger in the pie; and, as a result of this crude handling of human relations, Wilson wrecked his own career, ruined his health, shortened his life, caused America to stay out of the League, and altered the history of the world.

The famous publishing house of Doubleday Page always followed this rule: *Make the other person happy about doing the thing you suggest.* This firm was so expert at it that O. Henry declared that Doubleday Page could refuse one of his stories and do it with such graciousness, such appreciation, that he felt better when Doubleday refused a story than when another publisher accepted one.

I know a man who has to refuse many invitations to speak, invitations extended by friends, invitations coming from people to whom he is obligated; and yet he does it so adroitly that the other person is at least contented with his refusal. How does he do it? Not by merely talking about the fact that he is too busy and too this and too that. No, after expressing his appreciation of the invitation and regretting his inability to accept it, he suggests a substitute speaker. In other words, he doesn't give the other person any time to feel unhappy about the refusal. He immediately gets the other person thinking of some other speaker he may obtain.

"Why don't you get my friend, Cleveland Rodgers, the editor of the *Brooklyn Eagle,* to speak for you?" he will suggest. "Or have you thought about trying Guy Hickok? He lived in Paris fifteen years and has a lot of astonishing stories to tell about his experiences as a European correspondent. Or why not get Livingston Longfellow? He has some grand motion pictures of hunting big game in India."

J. A. Want, head of the J. A. Want Organization, one of the largest Hooven letter and photo-offset printing houses in New York, was faced with the necessity of changing a mechanic's attitude and demands without arousing resentment. This mechanic's job was to keep scores of typewriters and other hard-driven machines functioning smoothly night and day. He was always complaining that the hours were too long, that there was too much work, that he needed an assistant.

J. A. Want didn't give him an assistant, didn't give him shorter hours or less work, and yet he made the mechanic happy. How? This mechanic was given a private office. His name appeared on the door, and with it his title—"Manager of the Service Department."

He was no longer a repair man to be ordered about by every Tom, Dick, and Harry. He was now the manager of a department. He had dignity, recognition, a feeling of importance. He worked happily and without complaint.

Childish? Perhaps. But that is what they said to Napoleon when he created the Legion of Honor and distributed 1,500 crosses to his soldiers, and made eighteen of his generals "Marshals of France" and called his troops the "Grand Army." Napoleon was criticized for giving "toys" to war-hardened veterans, and Napoleon replied, "Men are ruled by toys."

This technique of giving titles and authority worked for Napoleon and it will work for you. For example, a friend of mine, Mrs. Gent of Scarsdale, New York, whom I've already mentioned, was troubled by boys running across and destroying her lawn. She tried criticism. She tried coaxing. Neither worked. Then she tried giving the worst sinner in the gang a title and a feeling of authority. She made him her "detective" and put him in charge of keeping all trespassers off her lawn. That solved her problem. Her "detective" built a bonfire in the backyard, heated an iron red hot, and threatened to burn any boy who stepped on the lawn.

Such is Human Nature.

So if you want to change people without arousing resentment or giving offense, **Rule 9** is:

Make the other person happy about the thing you suggest.

Nine Ways to Change People Without Giving Offense or Arousing Resentment

RULE 1: Begin with praise and honest appreciation.

RULE 2: Call attention to people's mistakes indirectly.

RULE 3: Talk about your own mistakes before criticizing the other person.

RULE 4: Ask questions instead of giving direct orders.

RULE 5: Let the other man save his face.

RULE 6: Praise the slightest improvement and praise every improvement. Be "hearty in your approbation and lavish in your praise."

RULE 7: Give the other person a fine reputation to live up to.

RULE 8: Use encouragement. Make the fault seem easy to correct.

RULE 9: Make the other person happy about doing the thing you suggest.

PART FIVE

Letters That Produce Miraculous Results

I'LL BET I KNOW what you are thinking now. You are probably saying to yourself something like this: " '*Letters that produce miraculous results!*' Absurd! Smacks of patent-medicine advertising!"

If you are thinking that, I don't blame you. I would probably have thought that myself if I had picked up a book like this fifteen years ago. Skeptical? Well, I like skeptical people. I spent the first twenty years of my life in Missouri—and I like people who have to be shown. Almost all the progress ever made in human thought has been made by the Doubting Thomases, the questioners, the challengers, the show-me crowd.

Let's be honest. Is the title, "Letters That Produce Miraculous Results," accurate?

No, to be frank with you, it isn't.

The truth is, it is a deliberate *understatement* of fact. Some of the letters reproduced in this chapter harvested results that were rated twice as good as miracles. Rated by whom? By Ken R. Dyke, one of the best-known sales promotion men in America, formerly sales promotion manager for Johns-Manvile, and now advertising manager for Colgate-Palmolive Peet Company and Chairman of the Board of the Association of National Advertisers.

Mr. Dyke says that letters he used to send out, asking for information from dealers, seldom brought more than a return of 5 to 8 per cent. He said he would have regarded a 15 per cent response as most extraordinary, and told me that, if his replies had ever soared to 20 percent, he would have regarded it as nothing short of a miracle.

But one of Mr. Dyke's letters, printed in this chapter, brought 42½ per cent; in other words, that letter was twice as good as a miracle. You can't laugh that off. And this letter wasn't a sport, a fluke, an accident. Similar results were obtained from scores of other letters.

How did he do it? Here is the explanation in Ken Dyke's own words: "This astonishing increase in the effectiveness of letters occurred immediately after I attended Mr. Carnegie's course in 'Effective Speaking and Human Relations.' I saw that the approach I had formerly used was all wrong. I tried to apply the principles taught in this book—and they resulted in an increase of from 500 to 800 per cent in the effectiveness of my letters asking for information."

Here is the letter. It pleases the other man by asking him to do the writer a small favor—a favor that makes him feel important.

My own comments on the letter appear in parentheses.

Mr. John Blank,
Blankville, Arizona.

Dear Mr. Blank,
    I wonder if you would mind helping me out of a little difficulty?

(Let's get the picture clear. Imagine a lumber dealer in Arizona receiving a letter from an executive of the Johns-Manville Company; and in the first line of the letter, this high-priced executive in New York asks the other fellow to help him out of a difficulty. I can imagine the dealer in Arizona saying to himself something like this: "Well, if this chap in New York is in trouble, he has certainly come to the right person. I always try to be generous and help people. Let's see what's wrong with him!")

Last year, I succeeded in convincing our company that what our dealers needed most to help increase their re-roofing sales was a year 'round direct-mail campaign paid for entirely by Johns-Manville.

(The dealer out in Arizona probably says, "Naturally, they ought to pay for it. They're hogging most of the profit as it is. They're making millions while I'm having hard scratchin' to pay the rent. . . . Now what is this fellow in trouble about?")

Recently I mailed a questionnaire to the 1,600 dealers who had used the plan and certainly was very much pleased with the hundreds of replies which showed that they appreciated this form of co-operation and found it most helpful.

On the strength of this, we have just released our new direct-mail plan which I know you'll like still better.

But this morning our president discussed with me my report of last year's plan and, as presidents will, asked me how much business I could trace to it. Naturally, I must come to you to help me answer him.

(That's a good phrase: "I must come to you to help me answer him." The big shot in New York is telling the truth, and he is giving the Johns-Manville dealer in Arizona honest, sincere recognition. Note that Ken Dyke doesn't waste any time talking about how important his company is. Instead, he immediately shows the other fellow how much he has to lean on him. Ken Dyke admits that he can't even make a report to the president of Johns-Manville without the dealer's help. Naturally, the dealer out in Arizona, being human, likes that kind of talk.)

> *What I'd like you to do is (1) to tell me, on the en-*
> *closed postcard, how many roofing and re-roofing jobs*
> *you feel last year's direct-mail plan helped you secure,*
> *and (2) give me, as nearly as you can, their total esti-*
> *mated value in dollars and cents (based on the total cost*
> *of the jobs applied).*

> *If you'll do this, I'll surely appreciate it and thank*
> *you for your kindness in giving me this information.*

> > *Sincerely,*
> > *Ken R. Dyke,*
> > *Sales Promotion Manager.*

(Note how, in the last paragraph, he whispers "I" and shouts "You." Note how generous he is in his praise: "surely appreciate," "thank you," "your kindness.")

Simple letter, isn't it? But it produced "miracles" by asking the other person to do a small favor—the performing of which gave him a feeling of importance.

That psychology will work, regardless of whether you are selling asbestos roofs or touring Europe in a Ford.

To illustrate. Homer Croy and I once lost our way while motoring through the interior of France. Halting our old Model T, we asked a group of peasants how we could get to the next big town.

The effect of the question was electrical. These peasants, wearing wooden shoes, regarded all Americans as rich. And automobiles were rare in those regions, extremely rare. Americans touring through France in a car! Surely we must be millionaires. Maybe cousins of Henry Ford. But they knew something we didn't know. We had more money than they had; but we had to come to them hat in hand to find out how to get to the next town. And that gave them a feeling of importance. They all started talking at once. One chap, thrilled at this rare opportunity, commanded the others to keep quiet. He wanted to enjoy all alone the thrill of directing us.

Try this yourself. The next time you are in a strange city, stop someone who is below you in the economic and social scale and say: "I wonder if you would mind helping me out of a little difficulty. Won't you please tell me how to get to such and such a place?"

Benjamin Franklin used this technique to turn a caustic enemy into a lifelong friend. Franklin, a young man at the time, had all his savings invested in a small printing business. He managed to get himself elected clerk of the General Assembly in Philadelphia. That position gave him the job of doing the official printing. There was good profit in this job, and Ben was eager to keep it. But a menace loomed ahead. One of the richest and ablest men in the Assembly disliked Franklin bitterly. He not only disliked Franklin, but he denounced him in a public talk.

That was dangerous, very dangerous. So Franklin resolved to make the man like him.

But how? That was a problem. By doing a favor for his enemy? No, that would have aroused his suspicions, maybe his contempt.

Franklin was too wise, too adroit to be caught in such a trap. So he did the very opposite. He asked his enemy to do him a favor.

Franklin didn't ask for a loan of ten dollars. No! No! Franklin asked a favor that pleased the other man—a favor that touched his vanity, a favor that gave him recognition, a favor that subtly expressed Franklin's admiration for his knowledge and achievements.

Here is the balance of the story in Franklin's own words:

Having heard that he had in his library a certain very scarce and curious book, I wrote a note to him, expressing my desire of perusing that book and requesting that he would do me the favor of lending it to me for a few days.

He sent it immediately, and I returned it in about a week with another note expressing strongly my sense of the favor.

When next we met in the House, he spoke to me (which he had never done before) and with great civility and he ever afterward manifested a readiness to serve me on all occasions, so that we became great friends and our friendship continued to his death.

Ben Franklin has been dead now for more than a hundred and fifty years, but the psychology that he used, the psychology of asking the other man to do you a favor, goes marching right on.

For example, it was used with remarkable success by one of my students, Albert B. Amsel. For years, Mr. Amsel, a salesman of plumbing and heating materials, had been trying to get the trade of a certain plumber in Brooklyn. This plumber's business was exceptionally large and his credit unusually good. But Amsel was licked from the beginning. The plumber was one of those disconcerting individuals who pride themselves on being rough, tough, and nasty. Sitting behind his desk with a big cigar tilted in the corner of his mouth, he snarled at Amsel every time he opened the door, "Don't need a thing today! Don't waste my time and yours! *Keep moving!*"

Then one day Mr. Amsel tried a new technique, a technique that split the account wide open, made a friend, and brought many fine orders.

Amsel's firm was negotiating for the purchase of a new branch store in Queens Village on Long Island. It was a neighborhood the plumber knew well, and one where he did a great deal of business. So this time, when Mr. Amsel called, he said: "Mr. C——, I'm not here to sell you anything today. I've got to ask you to do me a favor, if you will. Can you spare me just a minute of your time?"

"H'm—well," said the plumber, shifting his cigar. "What is on your mind? Shoot."

"My firm is thinking of opening up a branch store over in Queens Village," Mr. Amsel said. "Now, you know that locality as well as anyone living. So I've come to you to ask what you think about it. Is it a wise move—or not?"

Here was a new situation! For years this plumber had been getting his feeling of importance out of snarling at salesmen and ordering them to keep moving.

But here was a salesman begging him for advice; yes, a salesman from a big concern wanting his opinion as to what they should do.

"Sit down," he said, pulling forward a chair. And for

the next hour, he expatiated on the peculiar advantages and virtues of the plumbing market in Queens Village. He not only approved the location of the store, but he focused his intellect on outlining a complete course of action for the purchase of the property, the stocking of supplies, and the opening of trade. He got a feeling of importance by telling a wholesale plumbing concern how to run its business. From there, he expanded into personal grounds. He became friendly, and told Mr. Amsel of his intimate domestic difficulties and household wars.

"By the time I left that evening," Mr. Amsel says, "I not only had in my pocket a large initial order for equipment, but I had laid the foundations of a solid business friendship. I am playing golf now with this chap who formerly barked and snarled at me. This change in his attitude was brought about by my asking him to do me a little favor that made him feel important."

Let's examine another of Ken Dyke's letters, and again note how skillfully he applies this "do-me-a-favor" psychology.

A few years ago, Mr. Dyke was distressed at his inability to get business men, contractors, and architects to answer his letters asking for information.

In those days, he seldom got more than 1 per cent return from his letters to architects and engineers. He would have regarded 2 per cent as very good and 3 per cent as excellent. And 10 per cent? Why, 10 per cent would have been hailed as a miracle.

But the letter that follows pulled almost 50 per cent. . . . Five times as good as a miracle. And what replies! Letters of two and three pages! Letters glowing with friendly advice and co-operation.

Here is the letter. You will observe that in the psychology used—even in the phraseology in some places—the letter is almost identical with that quoted on page 219.

As you peruse this letter, read between the lines, try to analyze the feeling of the man who got it. Find out why it produced results five times as good as a miracle.

JOHNS-MANVILLE
22 East 40th Street
New York City

Mr. John Doe,
617 Doe Street,
Doeville, N. J.

Dear Mr. Doe:

I wonder if you'll help me out of a little difficulty?

About a year ago I persuaded our company that one of the things architects most needed was a catalogue which would give them the whole story of all J-M building materials and their part in repairing and remodeling homes.

The attached catalogue resulted—the first of its kind.

But now our stock is getting low, and when I mentioned it to our president he said (as presidents will) that he would have no objection to another edition *provided* I furnished satisfactory evidence that the catalogue had done the job for which it was designed.

Naturally, I must come to you for help, and I am therefore taking the liberty of asking you and forty-nine other architects in various parts of the country to be the jury.

To make it quite easy for you, I have written a few simple questions on the back of this letter. And I'll certainly regard it as a personal favor if you'll check the answers, add any comments that you may wish to make, and then slip this letter into the enclosed stamped envelope.

Needless to say, this won't obligate you in any way, and I now leave it to you to say whether the catalogue shall be discontinued or reprinted with improvements based on your experience and advice.

In any event, rest assured that I shall appreciate your co-operation very much. Thank you!

Sincerely yours,
Ken R. Dyke,
Sales Promotion Manager.

Another word of warning. I know from experience that some men, reading this letter, will try to use the same psychology mechanically. They will try to boost the other man's ego, not through genuine, real appreciation, but through flattery and insincerity. And their technique won't work.

Remember, we all crave appreciation and recognition, and will do almost anything to get it. But nobody wants insincerity. Nobody wants flattery.

Let me repeat: the principles taught in this book will work only when they come from the heart. I am not advocating a bag of tricks. I am talking about a new way of life.

PART SIX

Seven Rules For Making Your Home Life Happier

CHAPTER ONE

How to Dig Your Marital Grave in the Quickest Possible Way

SEVENTY-FIVE YEARS AGO, Napoleon III of France, nephew of Napoleon Bonaparte, fell in love with Marie Eugénie Ignace Augustine de Montijo, Countess of Teba, the most beautiful woman in the world—and married her. His advisors pointed out that she was only the daughter of an insignificant Spanish count. But Napoleon retorted: "What of it?" Her grace, her youth, her charm, her beauty filled him with divine felicity. In a speech hurled from the throne, he defied an entire nation: "I have preferred a woman I love and respect," he proclaimed, "to a woman unknown to me."

Napoleon and his bride had health, wealth, power, fame, beauty, love, adoration—all the requirements for a perfect romance. Never did the sacred fire of marriage glow with a brighter incandescence.

But, alas, the holy flame soon flickered and the incandescence cooled—and turned to embers. Napoleon could make Eugénie an empress; but nothing in all *la belle France,* neither the power of his love nor the might of his throne, could keep her from nagging.

Bedeviled by jealousy, devoured by suspicion, she flouted his orders, she denied him even a show of privacy. She broke into his office while he was engaged in affairs of state. She interrupted his most important discussions. She refused to leave him alone, always fearing that he might be consorting with another woman.

Often she ran to her sister, complaining of her husband, complaining, weeping, nagging, and threatening. Forcing her way into his study, she stormed at him and abused him. Napoleon, master of a dozen sumptuous palaces, Emperor of France, could not find a cupboard in which he could call his soul his own.

And what did Eugénie accomplish by all this?

Here is the answer. I am quoting now from E. A. Rheinhardt's engrossing book, *Napoleon and Eugénie: The Tragicomedy of an Empire:* "So it came about that Napoleon frequently would steal out by a little side door at night, with a soft hat pulled over his eyes, and, accompanied by one of his intimates, *really* betake himself to some fair lady who was expecting him, or else stroll about the great city as of old, passing through streets of the kind which an Emperor hardly sees outside a fairy tale, and breathing the atmosphere of might-have-beens."

That is what nagging accomplished for Eugénie. True, she sat on the throne of France. True, she was the most beautiful woman in the world. But neither royalty nor beauty can keep love alive amidst the poisonous fumes of nagging. Eugénie could have raised her voice like Job of old and have wailed: "The thing which I greatly feared is come upon me." Come upon her? She brought it upon herself, poor woman, by her jealousy and her nagging.

Of all the sure-fire, infernal devices ever invented by all the devils in hell for destroying love, nagging is the deadliest. It never fails. Like the bite of the king cobra, it always destroys, always kills.

The wife of Count Leo Tolstoi discovered that—after it was too late. Before she passed away, she confessed to her daughters: "I was the cause of your father's death." Her daughters didn't reply. They were both crying. They knew their mother was telling the truth. They knew she had killed him with her constant complaining, her eternal criticisms, and her eternal nagging.

Yet Count Tolstoi and his wife ought, by all odds, to have been happy. He was one of the most famous novelists of all time. Two of his masterpieces, *War and Peace* and *Anna Karenina,* will forever shine brightly among the literary glories of earth.

Tolstoi was so famous that his admirers followed him around day and night and took down in shorthand every word he uttered. Even if he merely said, "I guess I'll go to bed"; even trivial words like that, everything was written down; and now the Russian Government is printing every sentence that he ever wrote; and his combined writings will fill one hundred volumes.

In addition to fame, Tolstoi and his wife had wealth, social position, children. No marriage ever blossomed under softer skies. In the beginning, their happiness seemed too perfect, too intense, to endure. So kneeling together, they prayed to Almighty God to continue the ecstasy that was theirs.

Then an astonishing thing happened. Tolstoi gradually changed. He became a totally different person. He became ashamed of the great books that he had written, and from that time on he devoted his life to writing pamphlets preaching peace and the abolition of war and poverty.

This man who had once confessed that in his youth he had committed every sin imaginable—even murder—tried to follow literally the teachings of Jesus. He gave all his lands away and lived a life of poverty. He worked in the fields, chopping wood and pitching hay. He made his own shoes, swept his own room, ate out of a wooden bowl, and tried to love his enemies.

Leo Tolstoi's life was a tragedy, and the cause of his tragedy was his marriage. His wife loved luxury, but he despised it. She craved fame and the plaudits of society, but these frivolous things meant nothing whatever to him. She longed for money and riches, but he believed that wealth and private property were a sin.

For years, she nagged and scolded and screamed because he insisted on giving away the right to publish his books freely without paying him any royalties whatever. She wanted the money those books would produce.

When he opposed her, she threw herself into fits of hysteria, rolling on the floor with a bottle of opium at her lips, swearing that she was going to kill herself and threatening to jump down the well.

There is one event in their lives that to me is one of the most pathetic scenes in history. As I have already said, they were gloriously happy when they were first married; but now, forty-eight years later, he could hardly bear the sight of her. Sometimes of an evening, this old and heartbroken wife, starving for affection, came and knelt at his knees and begged him to read aloud to her the exquisite love passages that he had written about her in his diary fifty years previously. And as he read of those beautiful, happy days that were now gone forever, both of them wept. How different, how sharply different, the realities of life were from the romantic dreams they had once dreamed in the long ago.

Finally, when he was eighty-two years old, Tolstoi was unable to endure the tragic unhappiness of his home any longer, so he fled from his wife on a snowy October night in 1910—fled into the cold and darkness, not knowing where he was going.

Eleven days later, he died of pneumonia in a railway station. And his dying request was that she should not be permitted to come into his presence.

Such was the price Countess Tolstoi paid for her nagging and complaining and hysteria.

The reader may feel that she had much to nag about. Granted. But that is beside the point. The question is: did nagging help her, or did it make a bad matter infinitely worse?

"I really think I was insane." That is what Countess Tolstoi herself thought about it—after it was too late.

The great tragedy of Abraham Lincoln's life also was

his marriage. Not his assassination, mind you, but his marriage. When Booth fired, Lincoln never realized he had been shot; but he reaped almost daily, for twenty-three years, what Herndon, his law partner, described as "the bitter harvest of conjugal infelicity." "Conjugal infelicity?" That is putting it mildly. For almost a quarter of a century, Mrs. Lincoln nagged and harassed the life out of him.

She was always complaining, always criticizing her husband; nothing about him was ever right. He was stoop-shouldered, he walked awkwardly and lifted his feet straight up and down like an Indian. She complained that there was no spring to his step, no grace to his movement; and she mimicked his gait and nagged at him to walk with his toes pointed down, as she had been taught at Madame Mentelle's boarding school in Lexington.

She didn't like the way his huge ears stood out at right angles from his head. She even told him that his nose wasn't straight, that his lower lip stuck out, that he looked consumptive, that his feet and hands were too large, his head too small.

Abraham Lincoln and Mary Todd Lincoln were opposites in every way: in training, in background, in temperament, in tastes, in mental outlook. They irritated each other constantly.

"Mrs. Lincoln's loud, shrill voice," wrote the late Senator Albert J. Beveridge, the most distinguished Lincoln authority of this generation—"could be heard across the street, and her incessant outbursts of wrath were audible to all who lived near the house. Frequently her anger was displayed by other means than words, and accounts of her violence are numerous and unimpeachable."

To illustrate: Mr. and Mrs. Lincoln, shortly after their marriage, lived with Mrs. Jacob Early—a doctor's widow in Springfield who was forced to take in boarders.

One morning Mr. and Mrs. Lincoln were having breakfast when Lincoln did something that aroused the fiery temper of his wife. What, no one remembers now. But Mrs. Lincoln, in a rage, dashed a cup of hot coffee into her husband's face. And she did it in front of the other boarders.

Saying nothing, Lincoln sat there in humiliation and silence while Mrs. Early came with a wet towel and wiped off his face and clothes.

Mrs. Lincoln's jealousy was so foolish, so fierce, so incredible, that merely to read about some of the pathetic and disgraceful scenes she created in public—merely reading about them seventy-five years later makes one gasp with astonishment. She finally went insane; and perhaps the most charitable thing one can say about her is that her disposition was probably always affected by incipient insanity.

Did all this nagging and scolding and raging change Lincoln? In one way, yes. It certainly changed his attitude toward her. It made him regret his unfortunate marriage, and it made him avoid her presence as much as possible.

Springfield had eleven attorneys, and they couldn't all make a living there; so they used to ride horseback from one county seat to another, following Judge David Davis while he was holding court in various places. In that way, they managed to pick up business from all the county seat towns throughout the Eighth Judicial District.

The other attorneys always managed to get back to Springfield each Saturday and spend the week-end with their families. But Lincoln didn't. He dreaded to go home: and for three months in the spring, and again for three months in the autumn, he remained out on the circuit and never went near Springfield.

He kept this up year after year. Living conditions in the country hotels were often wretched; but, wretched as they were, he preferred them to his own home and Mrs. Lincoln's constant nagging and wild outbursts of temper.

Such are the results that Mrs. Lincoln, the Empress Eugénie, and Countess Tolstoi obtained by their nagging. They brought nothing but tragedy into their lives. They destroyed all that they cherished most.

Bessie Hamburger, who has spent eleven years in the Domestic Relations Court in New York City, and has reviewed thousands of cases of desertion, says that one of the chief reasons men leave home is because their wives nag.

Or, as the *Boston Post* puts it: "Many a wife has made her own marital grave with a series of little digs."

So, if you want to keep your home life happy, **Rule 1** is:

Don't, don't nag!!!

CHAPTER TWO

Love and Let Live

"I MAY COMMIT many follies in life," Disraeli said, "but I never intend to marry for love."

And he didn't. He stayed single until he was thirty-five, and then he proposed to a rich widow, a widow fifteen years his senior; a widow whose hair was white with the passing of fifty winters. Love? Oh, no. She knew he didn't love her. She knew he was marrying her for her money! So she made just one request; she asked him to wait a year to give her the opportunity to study his character. And at the end of that time, she married him.

Sounds pretty prosaic, pretty commercial, doesn't it? Yet paradoxically enough, Disraeli's marriage was one of the most glowing successes in all the battered and bespattered annals of matrimony.

The rich widow that Disraeli chose was neither young, nor beautiful, nor brilliant. Far from it. Her conversation bubbled with a laugh-provoking display of literary and historical blunders. For example, she "never knew which came first, the Greeks or the Romans." Her taste in clothes was bizarre; and her taste in house furnishings was fantastic. But she was a genius, a positive genius at the most important thing in marriage: the art of handling men.

She didn't attempt to set up her intellect against Disraeli's. When he came home bored and exhausted after an afternoon of matching repartee with witty duchesses, Mary Anne's frivolous patter permitted him to relax. Home, to his increasing delight, was a place where he could ease into his mental slippers and bask in the warmth of Mary Anne's adoration. These hours he spent at home with his aging wife were the happiest of his life. She was his helpmate, his confidante, his advisor. Every night he hurried home from the House of Commons to tell her the day's news. And—this is important—whatever he undertook, Mary Anne simply did not believe he could fail.

For thirty years, Mary Anne lived for Disraeli, and for him alone. Even her wealth she valued only because it made his life easier. In return, she was his heroine. He became an Earl after she died; but, even while he was still a commoner, he persuaded Queen Victoria to elevate Mary Anne to the peerage. And so, in 1868, she was made Viscountess Beaconsfield.

No matter how silly or scatterbrained she might appear in public, he never criticized her; he never uttered a word of reproach; and if anyone dared to ridicule her, he sprang to her defense with ferocious loyalty.

Mary Anne wasn't perfect, yet for three decades she never tired of talking about her husband, praising him, admiring him. Result? "We have been married thirty years," Disraeli said, "and I have never been bored by her." (Yet some people thought because Mary Anne didn't know history, she must be stupid!)

For his part, Disraeli never made it any secret that Mary Anne was the most important thing in his life. Result? "Thanks to his kindness," Mary Anne used to tell their friends, "my life has been simply one long scene of happiness."

Between them, they had a little joke. "You know," Disraeli would say, "I only married you for your money anyhow." And Mary Anne, smiling, would reply, "Yes, but if you had it to do over again, you'd marry me for love, wouldn't you?"

And he admitted it was true.

No, Mary Anne wasn't perfect. But Disraeli was wise enough to let her be herself.

As Henry James put it: "The first thing to learn in intercourse with others is noninterference with their own peculiar ways of being happy, provided those ways do not assume to interfere by violence with ours."

That's important enough to repeat: "The first thing to learn in intercourse with others is noninterference with their own peculiar ways of being happy. . . ."

Or, as Leland Foster Wood in his book, *Growing Together in the Family,* has observed: "Success in marriage is much more than a matter of finding the right person; it is also a matter of *being* the right person."

So, if you want your home life to be happy, **Rule 2** is:

Don't try to make your partner over.

CHAPTER THREE

Do This and You'll Be Looking Up the Time-tables to Reno

DISRAELI'S BITTEREST RIVAL in public life was the great Gladstone. These two clashed on every debatable subject under the Empire, yet they had one thing in common; the supreme happiness of their private lives.

William and Catherine Gladstone lived together for fifty-nine years, almost three score years glorified with an abiding devotion. I like to think of Gladstone, the most dignified of England's prime ministers, clasping his wife's hand and dancing around the hearthrug with her, singing this song:

"A ragamuffin husband and a rantipoling wife,
We'll fiddle it and scrape it through the ups and downs
of life."

Gladstone, a formidable enemy in public, never criticized at home. When he came down to breakfast in the morning, only to discover that the rest of his family was still sleeping, he had a gentle way of registering his reproach. He raised his voice and filled the house with a mysterious chant that reminded the other members that England's busiest man was waiting downstairs for his breakfast, all alone. Diplomatic, considerate, he rigorously refrained from domestic criticism.

And so, often, did Catherine the Great. Catherine ruled one of the largest empires the world has ever known. Over millions of her subjects she held the power of life and death. Politically, she was often a cruel tyrant, waging useless wars and sentencing scores of her enemies to be cut down by firing squads. Yet if the cook burned the meat, she said nothing. She smiled and ate it with a tolerance that the average American husband would do well to emulate.

Dorothy Dix, America's premier authority on the causes of marital unhappiness, declares that more than fifty per cent of all marriages are failures; and she knows that one of the reasons why so many romantic dreams break up on the rocks of Reno is criticism—futile, heartbreaking criticism.

So, you want to keep your home life happy, remember **Rule 3**:

Don't criticize.

And if you are tempted to criticize the children . . . you imagine I am going to say *don't*. But I am not. I am merely going to say, *before* you criticize them, read one of the classics of American journalism, "Father Forgets." It appeared originally as an editorial in the *People's Home Journal*. We are reprinting it here with the author's permission—reprinting it as it was condensed in the *Reader's Digest:*

"Father Forgets" is one of those little pieces which—dashed off in a moment of sincere feeling—strikes an echoing chord in so many readers as to become a perennial reprint favorite. Since its first appearance, some fifteen years ago, "Father Forgets" has been reproduced, writes the author, W. Livingston Larned, "in hundreds of magazines and house organs, and in newspapers the country over. It has been reprinted almost as extensively in many foreign languages. I have given personal permission to thousands who wished to read it from school, church, and lecture platforms. It has been 'on the air' on countless occasions and programs. Oddly enough, college periodicals have used it, and high-school magazines. Sometimes a little piece seems mysteriously to 'click.' This one certainly did."

FATHER FORGETS
W. LIVINGSTON LARNED

Listen, son: I am saying this as you lie asleep, one little paw crumpled under your cheek and the blond curls stickily wet on your damp forehead. I have stolen into your room alone. Just a few minutes ago, as I sat reading my paper in the library, a stifling wave of remorse swept over me. Guiltily I came to your bedside.

These are the things I was thinking, son: I had been cross to you. I scolded you as you were dressing for school because you gave your face merely a dab with a towel. I took you to task for not cleaning your shoes. I called out angrily when you threw some of your things on the floor.

At breakfast I found fault, too. You spilled things. You gulped down your food. You put your elbows on the table. You spread butter too thick on your bread. And as you started off to play and I made for my train, you turned and waved a hand and called, "Good-bye, Daddy!" and I frowned, and said in reply, "Hold your shoulders back!"

Then it began all over again in the late afternoon. As I came up the road I spied you, down on your knees, playing marbles. There were holes in your stockings. I humiliated you before your boy friends by marching you ahead of me to the house. Stockings were expensive—and if you had to buy them you would be more careful! Imagine that, son, from a father!

Do you remember, later, when I was reading in the library, how you came in, timidly, with a sort of hurt look in your eyes? When I glanced up over my paper, impatient at the interruption, you hesitated at the door. "What is it you want?" I snapped.

You said nothing, but ran across in one tempestuous plunge, and threw your arms around my neck and kissed me, and your small arms tightened with an affection that God had set blooming in your heart and which even neglect could not wither. And then you were gone, pattering up the stairs.

Well, son, it was shortly afterwards that my paper slipped from my hands and a terrible sickening fear came over me. What has habit been doing to me? The habit of finding fault, of reprimanding—this was my reward to you for being a boy. It was not that I did not love you; it was that I expected too much of youth. It was measuring you by the yardstick of my own years.

And there was so much that was good and fine and true in your character. The little heart of you was as big as the dawn itself over the wide hills. This was shown by your spontaneous impulse to rush in and kiss me good-night. Nothing else matters tonight, son. I have come to your bedside in the darkness, and I have knelt there, ashamed!

It is a feeble atonement; I know you would not understand these things if I told them to you during your waking hours. But tomorrow I will be a real daddy! I will chum with you, and suffer when you suffer, and laugh when you laugh. I will bite my tongue when impatient words come. I will keep saying as if it were a ritual: "He is nothing but a boy—a little boy!"

I am afraid I have visualized you as a man. Yet as I see you now, son, crumpled and weary in your cot, I see that you are still a baby. Yesterday you were in your mother's arms, your head on her shoulder. I have asked too much, too much.

CHAPTER FOUR

A Quick Way to Make Everybody Happy

"MOST MEN when seeking wives," says Paul Popenoe, Director of the Institute of Family Relations in Los Angeles, "are not looking for executives but for someone with allure and willingness to flatter their vanity and make them feel superior. Hence the woman office manager may be invited to luncheon, once. But she quite possibly dishes out warmed-over remnants of her college courses on 'main currents in contemporary philosophy,' and may even insist on paying her own bill. Result: she thereafter lunches alone.

"In contrast, the noncollegiate typist, when invited to luncheon, fixes an incandescent gaze on her escort and says yearningly. 'Now tell me some more about yourself.' Result: he tells the other fellows that 'she's no raving beauty, but I have never met a better talker.'"

Men should express their appreciation of a woman's effort to look well and dress becomingly. All men forget, if they have ever realized it, how profoundly women are interested in clothes. For example, if a man and a woman meet another man and woman on the street, the woman seldom looks at the other man; she usually looks to see how well the other woman is dressed.

My grandmother died a few years ago at the age of ninety-eight. Shortly before her death, we showed her a photograph of herself that had been taken a third of a century earlier. Her failing eyes couldn't see the picture very well, and the only question she asked was: "What dress did I have on?" Think of it! An old woman in her last December, bedridden, weary with age as she lay within the shadow of the century mark, her memory fading so fast that she was no longer able to recognize even her own daughters, still interested in knowing what dress she had worn a third of a century before! I was at her bedside when she asked that question. It left an impression on me that will never fade.

The men who are reading these lines can't remember what suits or shirts they wore five years ago, and they haven't the remotest desire to remember them. But women —they are different, and we American men ought to recognize it. French boys of the upper class are trained to express their admiration of a woman's frock and *chapeau,* not only once but many times during an evening. And fifty million Frenchmen can't be wrong!

I have among my clippings a story that I know never happened, but it illustrates a truth, so I'll repeat it:

According to this silly story, a farm woman, at the end of a heavy day's work, set before her men folks a heaping pile of hay. And when they indignantly demanded whether she'd gone crazy, she replied: "Why, how did I know you'd notice? I've been cooking for you men for the last twenty years, and in all that time I ain't heard no word to let me know you *wasn't* just eating hay!"

The pampered aristocrats of Moscow and St. Petersburg used to have better manners; in the Russia of the Czars, it was the custom of the upper classes, when they had enjoyed a fine dinner, to insist on having the cook brought into the dining room to receive their congratulations.

Why not have as much consideration for your wife? The next time the fried chicken is done to a tender turn, tell her so. Let her know that you appreciate the fact that you're not just eating hay. Or, as Texas Guinan used to say, "Give the little girl a great big hand."

And while you're about it, don't be afraid to let her know how important she is to your happiness. Disraeli was as great a statesman as England ever produced; yet, as we've seen, he wasn't ashamed to let the world know how much he "owed to the little woman."

Just the other day, while perusing a magazine, I came across this. It's from an interview with Eddie Cantor.

"I owe more to my wife," says Eddie Cantor, "than to anyone else in the world. She was my best pal as a boy; she helped me to go straight. And after we married she saved every dollar, and invested it, and reinvested it. She built up a fortune for me. We have five lovely children. And she's made a wonderful home for me always. If I've gotten anywhere, give her the credit."

Out in Hollywood, where marriage is a risk that even Lloyd's of London wouldn't take a gamble on, one of the few outstandingly happy marriages is that of Warner Baxter's. Mrs. Baxter, the former Winifred Bryson, gave up a brilliant stage career when she married. Yet her sacrifice has never been permitted to mar their happiness. "She missed the applause of stage success," Warner Baxter says, "but I have tried to see that she is entirely aware of *my* applause. If a woman is to find happiness at all in her husband, she is to find it in his appreciation and devotion. If that appreciation and devotion is actual, there is the answer to *his* happiness also."

There you are.

So, if you want to keep your home life happy, one of the most important rules is **Rule 4**:

Give honest appreciation.

CHAPTER FIVE

They Mean So Much
to a Woman

FROM TIME IMMEMORIAL, flowers have been considered the language of love. They don't cost much, especially in season, and often they're for sale on the street corners. Yet, considering the rarity with which the average husband takes home a bunch of daffodils, you might suppose them to be as expensive as orchids and as hard to come by as the edelweiss which flowers on the cloud-swept cliffs of the Alps.

Why wait until your wife goes to the hospital to give her a few flowers? Why not bring her a few roses tomorrow night? You like to experiment. Try it. See what happens.

George M. Cohan, busy as he was on Broadway, used to telephone his mother twice a day up to the time of her death. Do you suppose he had startling news for her each time? No, the meaning of little attentions is this: it shows the person you love that you are thinking of her, that you want to please her, and that her happiness and welfare are very dear, and very near, to your heart.

Women attach a lot of importance to birthdays and anniversaries—just why, will forever remain one of those feminine mysteries. The average man can blunder through life without memorizing many dates, but there are a few which are indispensable: 1492, 1776, the date of his wife's birthday, and the year and date of his own marriage. If need be, he can even get along without the first two—but not the last!

Judge Joseph Sabbath of Chicago, who has reviewed 40,000 marital disputes and reconciled 2,000 couples, says: "Trivialities are at the bottom of most marital unhappiness. Such a simple thing as a wife's waving good-by to her husband when he goes to work in the morning would avert a good many divorces."

Robert Browning, whose life with Elizabeth Barrett Browning was perhaps the most idyllic on record, was never too busy to keep love alive with little tributes and attentions. He treated his invalid wife with such consideration that she once wrote to her sisters: "And now I begin to wonder naturally whether I may not be some sort of real angel after all."

Too many men underestimate the value of these small, every day attentions. As Gaynor Maddox said in an article in the *Pictorial Review:* "The American home really needs a few new vices. Breakfast in bed, for instance, is one of those amiable dissipations a greater number of women should be indulged in. Breakfast in bed to a woman does much the same thing as a private club for a man."

That's what marriage is in the long run—a series of trivial incidents. And woe to the couple who overlook that fact. Edna St. Vincent Millay summed it all up once in one of her concise little rhymes:

> " '*Tis not love's going hurts my days,*
> *But that it went in little ways.*"

That's a good verse to memorize. Out in Reno, the courts grant divorces six days a week, at the rate of one every ten marriages. How many of these marriages do you suppose were wrecked upon the reef of real tragedy? Mighty few, I'll warrant. If you could sit there day in, day out, listening to the testimony of those unhappy husbands and wives, you'd know love "went in little ways."

Take your pocket knife now and cut out this quotation. Paste it inside your hat or paste it on the mirror, where you will see it every morning when you shave:

"I shall pass this way but once; any good, therefore, that a can do or any kindness that I can show to any human being, let me do it now. Let me not defer nor neglect it, for I shall not pass this way again."

So, if you want to keep your home life happy, **Rule 5** is:

Pay little attentions.

CHAPTER SIX

If You Want to Be Happy,
Don't Neglect This One

WALTER DAMROSCH married the daughter of James G. Blaine, one of America's greatest orators and one-time candidate for President. Ever since they met many years ago at Andrew Carnegie's home in Scotland, the Damrosches have led a conspicuously happy life.

The secret?

"Next to care in choosing a partner," says Mrs. Damrosch, "I should place courtesy after marriage. If young wives would only be as courteous to their husbands as to strangers! Any man will run from a shrewish tongue."

Rudeness is the cancer that devours love. Everyone knows this, yet it's notorious that we are more polite to strangers than we are to our own relatives.

We wouldn't dream of interrupting strangers to say, "Good heavens, are you going to tell that old story again!" We wouldn't dream of opening our friends' mail without permission, or prying into their personal secrets. And it's only the members of our own family, those who are nearest

247

and dearest to us, that we dare insult for their trivial faults.

Again to quote Dorothy Dix: "It is an amazing but true thing that practically the only people who ever say mean, insulting, wounding things to us are those of our own households."

"Courtesy," says Henry Clay Risner, "is that quality of heart that overlooks the broken gate and calls attention to the flowers in the yard beyond the gate."

Courtesy is just as important to marriage as oil is to your motor.

Oliver Wendell Holmes, the beloved "Autocrat of the Breakfast Table," was anything but an autocrat in his own home. In fact, he carried his consideration so far that when he felt melancholy and depressed, he tried to conceal his blues from the rest of his family. It was bad enough for him to have to bear them himself, he said, without inflicting them on the others as well.

That is what Oliver Wendell Holmes did. But what about the average mortal? Things go wrong at the office; he loses a sale or gets called on the carpet by the boss. He develops a devastating headache or misses the five-fifteen; and he can hardly wait till he gets home—to take it out on the family.

In Holland you leave your shoes outside on the doorstep before you enter the house. By the Lord Harry, we could learn a lesson from the Dutch and shed our workaday troubles before we enter our homes.

William James once wrote an essay called "On a Certain Blindness in Human Beings." It would be worth a special trip to your nearest library to get that essay and read it. "Now the blindness in human beings of which this discourse will treat," he wrote, "is the blindness with which we all are afflicted in regard to the feelings of creatures and people different from ourselves."

"The blindness with which we all are afflicted." Many men who wouldn't dream of speaking sharply to a customer, or even to their partners in business, think nothing of barking at their wives. Yet, for their personal happiness, marriage is far more important to them, far more vital, than business.

The average man who is happily married is happier by far than the genius who lives in solitude. Turgenev, the great Russian novelist, was acclaimed all over the civilized world. Yet he said: "I would give up all my genius, and all my books, if there were only some woman, somewhere, who cared whether or not I came home late for dinner."

What are the chances of happiness in marriage anyway? Dorothy Dix, as we have already said, believes that more than half of them are failures; but Dr. Paul Popenoe thinks otherwise. He says: "A man has a better chance of succeeding in marriage than any other enterprise he may go into. Of all the man that go into the grocery business, 70 per cent fail. Of the men and women who enter matrimony, 70 per cent succeed."

Dorothy Dix sums the whole thing up like this:

"Compared with marriage," she says, "being born is a mere episode in our careers, and dying a trivial incident.

"No woman can ever understand why a man doesn't put forth the same effort to make his home a going concern as he does to make his business or profession a success.

"But, althought to have a contented wife and a peaceful and happy home means more to a man than to make a million dollars, not one man in a hundred ever gives any real serious thought or makes any honest effort to make his marriage a success. He leaves the most important thing in his life to chance, and he wins out or loses, according to whether fortune is with him or not. Women can never understand why their husbands refuse to handle them diplomatically, when it would be money in their pockets to use the velvet glove instead of the strongarm method.

"Every man knows that he can jolly his wife into doing anything, and doing without anything. He knows that if he hands her a few cheap compliments about what a wonderful manager she is, and how she helps him, she will squeeze every nickle. Every man knows that if he tells his wife how beautiful and lovely she looks in her last year's dress, she wouldn't trade it for the latest Paris importation. Every man knows that he can kiss his wife's eyes shut until she will be

blind as a bat, and that he has only to give her a warm
smack on the lips to make her dumb as an oyster.

"And every wife knows that her husband knows these
things about her, because she has furnished him with a
complete diagram about how to work her. And she never
knows whether to be mad at him or disgusted with him,
because he would rather fight with her and pay for it in
having to eat bad meals, and have his money wasted, and
buy her new frocks and limousines and pearls, than to take
the trouble to flatter her a little and treat her the way she is
begging to be treated."

So, if you want to keep your home life happy, **Rule 6** is:

Be courteous.

CHAPTER SEVEN

Don't Be
a "Marriage Illiterate"

DR. KATHARINE BEMENT DAVIS, general secretary of the Bureau of Social Hygiene, once induced a thousand married women to reply very frankly to a set of intimate questions. The result was shocking—an incredibly shocking comment upon the sexual unhappiness of the average American adult. After perusing the answers she received from these thousand married women, Dr. Davis published without hesitation her conviction that one of the chief causes of divorce in this country is physical mismating.

Dr. G. V. Hamilton's survey verifies this finding. Dr. Hamilton spent four years studying the marriages of one hundred men and one hundred women. He asked these men and women individually something like four hundred questions concerning their married lives, and discussed their problems exhaustively—so exhaustively that the whole investigation took four years. This work was considered so important sociologically that it was financed by a group of leading philanthropists. You can read the results of the

...periment in *What's Wrong with Marriage?* by George
J. V. Hamilton and Kenneth Macgowan.

Well, what *is* wrong with marriage? "It would take a very
prejudiced and very reckless psychiatrist," says Dr. Hamilton, "to say that most married friction doesn't find its
source in sexual maladjustment. At any rate, the frictions
which arise from other difficulties would be ignored in
many, many cases if the sexual relation itself were satisfactory."

Dr. Paul Popenoe, as head of the Institute of Family Relations in Los Angeles, has reviewed thousands of marriages
and he is one of America's foremost authorities on home
life. According to Dr. Popenoe, failure in marriage is
usually due to four causes. He lists them in this order:

1. Sexual maladjustment.
2. Difference of opinion as to the way of spending
   leisure time.
3. Financial difficulties.
4. Mental, physical, or emotional abnormalities.

Notice that sex comes first; and that, strangely enough,
money difficulties come only third on the list.

All authorities on divorce agree upon the absolute necessity for sexual compatibility. For example, a few years ago
Judge Hoffman of the Domestic Relations Court of Cin-
cinnati—a man who has listened to thousands of domestic
tragedies—announced: "Nine out of ten divorces are
caused by sexual troubles."

"Sex," says the famous psychologist, John B. Watson, "is
admittedly the most important subject in life. It is admittedly the thing which causes the most ship-wrecks in the
happiness of men and women."

And I have heard a number of practicing physicians in
speeches before my own classes say practically the same
thing. Isn't it pitiful, then, that in the twentieth century,
with all of our books and all of our education, marriages
should be destroyed and lives wrecked by ignorance concerning this most primal and natural instinct?

The Rev. Oliver M. Butterfield after eighteen years as a Methodist minister gave up his pulpit to direct the Family Guidance Service in New York City, and he has probably married as many young people as any man living. He says:

"Early in my experience as a minister I discovered that, in spite of romance and good intentions, many couples who come to the marriage altar are matrimonial illiterates."

Matrimonial illiterates!

And he continues: "When you consider that we leave the highly difficult adjustment of marriage so largely to chance, the marvel is that our divorce rate is only 16 per cent. An appalling number of husbands and wives are not really married but simply undivorced: they live in a sort of purgatory."

"Happy marriages," says Dr. Butterfield, "are rarely the product of chance: they are architectural in that they are intelligently and deliberately planned."

To assist in this planning, Dr. Butterfield has for years insisted that any couple he marries must discuss with him frankly their plans for the future. And it was as a result of these discussions that he came to the conclusion that so many of the high contracting parties were "matrimonial illiterates."

"Sex," says Dr. Butterfield, "is but one of the many satisfactions in married life, but unless this relationship is right, nothing else can be right."

But how to get it right?

"Sentimental reticence"—I'm still quoting Dr. Butterfield—"must be replaced by an ability to discuss objectively and with detachment attitudes and practices of married life. There is no way in which this ability can be better acquired than through a book of sound learning and good taste. I keep on hand several of these books in addition to a supply of my booklet, *Marriage and Sexual Harmony*.

"Of all the books that are available, the two that seem to me most satisfactory for general reading are: *The Sex Technique in Marriage* by Isabel E. Hutton and *The Sexual Side of Marriage* by Max Exner."

So **Rule 7** of "How to Make Your Home Life Happier" is:

Read a good book on the sexual side of marriage.

Learn about sex from books? Why not? A few years ago, Columbia University, together with the American Social Hygiene Association, invited leading educators to come and discuss the sex and marriage problems of college students. At that conference, Dr. Paul Popenoe said: "Divorce is on the decrease. And one of the reasons it is on the decrease is that people are reading more of the recognized books on sex and marriage."

So I sincerely feel that I have no right to complete a chapter on "How to Make Your Home Life Happier" without recommending a list of books that deal frankly and in a scientific manner with this tragic problem.

HARD COVER

Ideal Marriage, by Theodore Hendrik Van de Velde, M.D. Random House, 201 East 50th Street, New York City.

The Sexual Side of Marriage, by M. J. Exner, M.D. W. W. Norton & Company, Inc., 500 Fifth Avenue, New York City.

Preparation for Marriage, by Ernest R. Groves. Emerson Books, Inc., Reynolds Lane, Buchanan, N.Y.

PAPERBACK

First Aid for the Happy Marriage, by Rebecca O. Liswood, M.D. Pocket Books, 630 Fifth Avenue, New York City.

Sexual Feeling in Married Men and Women, by G. Lombard Kelly, M.D. Pocket Books, 630 Fifth Avenue, New York City.

Sexual Pleasure in Marriage, by Jerome and Julia Rainer. Pocket Books, 630 Fifth Avenue, New York City.

IN A NUTSHELL

Seven Rules For Making Your Home Life Happier

RULE 1: Don't nag.

RULE 2: Don't try to make your partner over.

RULE 3: Don't criticize.

RULE 4: Give honest appreciation.

RULE 5: Pay little attentions.

RULE 6: Be courteous.

RULE 7: Read a good book on the sexual side of marriage.

In its issue for June 1933, *American Magazine* printed an article by Emmet Crozier, "Why Marriages Go Wrong." The following is a questionnaire reprinted from that article. You may find it worth while to answer these questions, giving yourself ten points for each question you can answer in the affirmative.

For Husbands

1. Do you still "court" your wife with an occasional gift of flowers, with remembrances of her birthday and wedding anniversary, or with some unexpected attention, some unlooked-for tenderness?

2. Are you careful never to criticize her before others?

3. Do you give her money to spend entirely as she chooses, above the household expenses?

4. Do you make an effort to understand her varying feminine moods and help her through periods of fatigue, nerves, and irritability?

5. Do you share at least half of your recreation hours with your wife?

6. Do you tactfully refrain from comparing your wife's cooking or housekeeping with that of your mother or of Bill Jones' wife, except to her advantage?

7. Do you take a definite interest in her intellectual life, her clubs and societies, the books she reads, her views on civic problems?

8. Can you let her dance with and receive friendly attentions from other men without making jealous remarks?

9. Do you keep alert for opportunities to praise her and express your admiration for her?

10. Do you thank her for the little jobs she does for you, such as sewing on a button, darning your socks, and sending your clothes to the cleaners?

For Wives

1. Do you give your husband complete freedom in his business affairs, and do you refrain from criticizing his associates, his choice of a secretary, or the hours he keeps?
2. Do you try your best to make your home interesting and attractive?
3. Do you vary the household menu so that he never quite knows what to expect when he sits down to the table?
4. Do you have an intelligent grasp of your husband's business so you can discuss it with him helpfully?
5. Can you meet financial reverses bravely, cheerfully, without criticizing your husband for his mistakes or comparing him unfavorably with more successful men?
6. Do you make a special effort to get along amiably with his mother or other relatives?
7. Do you dress with an eye for your husband's likes and dislikes in color and style?
8. Do you compromise little differences of opinion in the interest of harmony?
9. Do you make an effort to learn games your husband likes, so you can share his leisure hours?
10. Do you keep track of the day's news, the new books, and new ideas, so you can hold your husband's intellectual interests?

Index